TONY EVANS

PRAYING
like a
KINGDOM
HERO

HARVEST HOUSE PUBLISHERS
EUGENE, OREGON

Cover design by Bryce Williamson

Cover photo © Foryou13 / Gettyimages

Interior design by Rockwell Davis

The prayers in this book were inspired by Dr. Evans's teaching but were written with the help of his writing assistant, Heather Hair.

For bulk, special sales, or ministry purchases, please call 1-800-547-8979. Email: Customerservice@hhpbooks.com

is a federally registered trademark of The Hawkins Children's LLC. Harvest House Publishers, Inc., is the exclusive licensee of the trademark.

Praying Like a Kingdom Hero

Copyright © 2022 by Tony Evans
Published by Harvest House Publishers
Eugene, Oregon 97408
www.harvesthousepublishers.com

ISBN 978-0-7369-8446-1 (pbk.)
ISBN 978-0-7369-8447-8 (eBook)

Library of Congress Control Number: 2021937790

Printed in the United States of America

22 23 24 25 26 27 28 29 30 / BP / 10 9 8 7 6 5 4 3 2 1

Acknowledgments

I want to thank my friends at Harvest House Publishers for their long-standing partnership in bringing my thoughts, study, and words to print. I particularly want to thank Bob Hawkins for his friendship over the years, as well as his pursuit of excellence in leading his company. I also want to publicly thank Kim Moore and Jean Bloom for their help in the editorial process. In addition, my appreciation goes out to Heather Hair for her skills and insights in collaboration on this manuscript.

CONTENTS

A Kingdom Hero's Journey Through Prayer   9

1. Praying for Increased Helpfulness   13

2. Praying for Greater Consistency   15

3. Praying to Become a Better Friend   17

4. Praying for Relational Commitment   21

5. Praying for Direction in Vocation   25

6. Praying for Bravery.   27

7. Praying for Honesty.   29

8. Praying for Personal Strength.   31

9. Praying to Develop Tenacity   35

10. Praying for Courage   37

11. Praying to Inspire Others.   39

12. Praying for Guidance.   41

13. Praying for a Strong Moral Compass.   45

14. Praying for Relational Competence.   49

15. Praying for Developed Skills and Talents   51

16. Praying for Spiritual Strength   53

17. Praying for Developed Spiritual Gifts   55

18. Praying for Empathy   57

19. Praying for Purposeful Speech   59

20. Praying for a Greater Awareness of What Others Face 61

21. Praying for the Spiritual Gift of Mercy. 63

22. Praying for Personal Confidence 67

23. Praying for Confidence in God 71

24. Praying for the Ability to Forgive 73

25. Praying for the Ability to Apologize 77

26. Praying for Tools to Overcome Anxiety 79

27. Praying for an Increased Ability to Care 81

28. Praying for the Will to Live Up to My Potential 83

29. Praying for Deeper Faith 87

30. Praying for Experiences That Will Grow My Faith 89

31. Praying for Opportunities to Witness God's Power 93

32. Praying for Strength During Struggles 95

33. Praying for Peace for Our Planet 97

34. Praying for Kingdom Values 99

35. Praying for Open Doors to Serve 101

36. Praying for Faithfulness 103

37. Praying for a Positive Mindset 105

38. Praying for a Willingness to Take Risks 109

39. Praying for Resilience to Overcome Setbacks 111

40. Praying for Persistence 115

41. Praying for Good Things 117

42. Praying for Assurance 119

43. Praying for Physical Strength 123

44. Praying for Excellent Health 127

45. Praying for Mental Clarity......................... 129

46. Praying for Spiritual Clarity....................... 131

47. Praying for More Love............................ 133

48. Praying for Spiritual Maturity 137

49. Praying for More Time in God's Word 141

50. Praying for Greater Opportunities for Evangelism 145

51. Praying for Insight into Biblical Justice 149

52. Praying for Intimacy with God 151

53. Praying for Boldness in My Speech 155

54. Praying for Self-Control 159

55. Praying for Assurance of Direction 163

56. Praying for Personal Peace 167

57. Praying for Blessing 169

58. Praying for Kingdom Impact 171

59. Praying for Discernment 175

60. Praying for the Power from God's Word 177

   Appendix: The Urban Alternative.................... 181

A KINGDOM HERO'S JOURNEY THROUGH PRAYER

God created you on purpose for a purpose. You have a calling to fulfill. As you live out your purpose, you will find yourself making choices and exhibiting character qualities reflective of those named as kingdom heroes in Scripture. This is because the general makeup of a kingdom hero reflects and resembles God's character and heart. Living as a kingdom hero means living under and according to God's rule over every aspect of your life.

In this book, *Praying Like a Kingdom Hero*, I've given you a multitude of guided prayers to help you explore these heroic kingdom qualities and character traits so you can develop and increase their existence in your own life. These prayers have been crafted to walk you through many characteristics of kingdom living simultaneously, so you will come to know them and learn to develop them more in your daily living. As you go through this book, I hope your understanding of God's purpose for your life will become clearer, thus enabling you to live out your calling of advancing His kingdom agenda on earth.

Numerous kingdom hero character qualities and traits are found in Scripture, and each one relates to an expression of God's heart through humanity. As you pray prayers based on kingdom virtues, you come to know these qualities and traits more and apply them in your own life. As a result, you will also come to experience God's love and power infused in you on a higher level than ever before.

To help facilitate your prayers for kingdom hero qualities and traits to be made manifest more fully in your life, I've provided four prayers related to each of the main ones found in kingdom heroes in the Word of God. Prayer is heavenly permission for earthly interference. Prayer is communication with God. He longs to be involved with you on a personal level, and prayer opens the door for this to happen. I encourage you to pray regularly, because abiding with God through prayer is one of the most important things you can do in life.

As in many of my guided-prayer books, each prayer has four sections based on the prayer acronym ACTS. This prayer acronym is not a magic formula; rather, it provides structure so our prayers can cover important aspects of communication with God: Adoration, Confession, Thanksgiving, and Supplication.

You can pray these guided prayers word for word, or you can use them as a springboard to your own prayers directed toward the attributes or personal qualities of God you're praying about. Or you can pray a combination of the two. It doesn't matter. What matters is that you pray.

I also encourage you to use this book to help you focus more intently on getting to know God Himself more fully. As you do, you can follow this helpful outline to nurture your time with Him:

> **Identify** a time each day when you can spend concentrated and focused energy on pursuing a greater relationship with God.

> **Consider** several ways to nurture your relationship with God during this time. It could be freely writing thoughts you have toward Him or thanking Him for any of His attributes in a journal. Or it could be looking up Scripture on a given attribute of God and meditating on it for a few minutes.

Evaluate how your relationship deepens as you spend consistent time with God in His Word and with Him in prayer. Also assess whether praying these prayers makes it easier for you to proclaim Jesus to others through your words and actions. That should be a natural outgrowth of knowing God's heart more deeply.

Repeat this practice. After you've put it into play for at least a week, continue to incorporate the various prayers into your daily intimate time with God.

Knowing God's heart and the kingdom qualities He wants you to live out will bring you stability in times of crisis and change. We've gone through a significant number of difficulties and challenges in our culture over the last few years, and everyone could use more calm in their hearts. This guided-prayer book has been designed with the hope that it will bring you just that—calm. As you get to know God through relational communication with Him, may He reveal Himself more fully to you and give you greater grace and peace each day. May He empower you to live as the true kingdom hero He has designed you to be.

PRAYING FOR INCREASED HELPFULNESS

*Now we who are strong ought to bear the weaknesses of those
without strength and not just please ourselves. Each of us
is to please his neighbor for his good, to his edification.*

ROMANS 15:1-2

Adoration

Heavenly Father, You are the model for what it means to be a kingdom hero. You exist above and beyond all the virtues and character qualities that embody our definition and understanding of heroes. Reliance as a friend is one of these qualities. The ability to be found faithful and helpful in times of need defines a hero, and it defines You entirely.

You are always present and able to help in times of trouble. I praise You and lift up Your name to glorify You for Your dependability and helpfulness to me when I need You the most. Just knowing You are there enables me to find the courage I need to get through each day with strength and resilience.

Confession

God, I confess that I don't reflect Your image as frequently as I wish I did. I can see how You are. I can see the level of helpfulness You provide to those under Your care, and I worship You for that.

I want to be a greater representation of You in all that I do, but I don't always or even frequently rise to that level. Forgive me for falling short of living my life as the kingdom hero You have designed and created me to be, particularly in this area of being helpful to those who need me and can benefit from what I have to offer them.

Thanksgiving

Thank You, God, that I can grow and develop the various qualities that will place me more into living as a kingdom hero. Thank You that I'm not stuck at the level of maturity or discipleship where I find myself today. I can become more helpful to those around me. I can learn to look outward more than inward for what needs I seek to meet.

Thank You that I can grow with Your love and care in my life, and that I can experience the fullness of the destiny You have planned for me. I'm not stuck. Through Your gracious help in my own life, I can become more helpful to others in need.

Supplication

God, I want to live my life as a kingdom hero who reflects Your interest in others through a display of consistent helpfulness to those in need. Give me more opportunities to develop this relational skill. Open my heart to be more attuned to the needs of those around me so I can be aware of how I can help others more regularly. Show me what it means to live with this quality, and enable me to live up to my own hopes and desires in how I want to help others. When people who know me think of someone who is helpful, I want that person to be me.

I ask that You give me this opportunity. I ask for Your guidance on how to be more effective as a kingdom hero who is advancing Your kingdom agenda on earth.

In Christ's name I pray, amen.

2

PRAYING FOR GREATER CONSISTENCY

Therefore, my beloved brethren, be steadfast, immovable,
always abounding in the work of the Lord, knowing
that your toil is not in vain in the Lord.

1 CORINTHIANS 15:58

Adoration

God, consistency is the definition of Your character. Without consistency for even a moment, the world would unravel. The earth would spin off its axis. The oxygen would cease to be exactly as we need it to be.

You are the epitome of consistency. You are the sum total of consistency. I honor this quality of Yours as I realize how much I depend on You and Your consistency. This heroic trait supplies life to all of us. I worship You for Your ability to remain so consistent in all You are and in all You do on behalf of all of us who live within the design of Your world.

Confession

Heavenly Father, if I had a fraction of Your consistency, I would live my life as a kingdom hero on such a greater level. I confess that I'm not always reliable. I aim to be consistent, but sometimes I'm distracted or my emotions get the best of me. Then I give in to how I'm feeling rather than act on what I know I need in the moment.

Forgive me for my failure at times to model consistency in my character, emotions, and even goals. I know this can negatively impact my relationships, and I don't want that to happen. I want to improve in this quality, Lord, so that my life will resemble that of a kingdom hero on a more consistent basis.

Thanksgiving

Heavenly Father, thank You for the grace You show toward me as I seek to live my life as a kingdom hero. Thank You for demonstrating the critical nature of consistency in a believer's life. Thank You for always showing up when You are needed and for providing all I need in order to live my life to the fullest.

Please receive my thanksgiving, attached to it the hope that I will increase my level of spiritual consistency and demonstration of kingdom values. I want to be more helpful to those around me. I want to be more influential on the culture at large as well as in my local community of Christ-followers.

Supplication

God, I ask for opportunities to learn the art of living consistently as a kingdom hero in the various areas of my life. Will You give me time to grow in my consistency as a leader? Will You reveal to me how I can develop greater consistency in my study of Your Word and in time spent with You? Will You enable me to identify those areas in my life that would be improved by applying a greater consistency of effort, focus, and diligence?

I ask for Your hand to guide me and for Your heart to inspire me as I grow more consistent in my walk as a kingdom follower. I want to impact the world with Your kingdom agenda in all that I do.

In Jesus' name I pray, amen.

PRAYING TO BECOME A BETTER FRIEND

*Oil and perfume make the heart glad, so a
man's counsel is sweet to his friend.*

PROVERBS 27:9

Adoration

Lord God, the greatest model of true friendship is the life of Christ when He walked among us on earth and then gave His life so that we may live for eternity. To those who place their faith in Him for the forgiveness of sins, He gives eternal life.

I praise You for this reflection of Your heart modeled for us in Jesus Christ. I honor Your ability to love without expecting anything in return. I worship You for the depth of Your love revealed time and time again, showing each of us what it means to truly live as a kingdom hero. You are my greatest friend, and I want to reflect You in all of my relationships so that others can come to know You more fully as they interact with me.

Confession

God, I have not always been a great friend, especially when I haven't seen the relationship as beneficial to me in some way. I want to be a better friend because I know that is one definition of a kingdom hero. Kingdom heroes seek to reflect Your values and attributes in all they do. Being a better friend to those around me is part of identifying with Christ, and it's part of His life being made manifest through my own.

Forgive me for letting others down in the past—whether they've been family members, coworkers, neighbors, or friends. Forgive me for focusing on myself and what I wanted or what I felt I needed more than looking out for the needs of others.

Thanksgiving

God, thank You for bringing this area of personal growth and development to the forefront of my mind through these guided prayers. I do want to be a better friend, and I want to be someone to whom others look for sound biblical counsel.

Thank You for giving me the awareness to pray for needs. I know that, through prayer, I will grow in this area. Thank You for Your Word. It gives me the foundation I need to grow in wisdom so I can guide others on the path they should take according to Your Word. Thank You for the freedom I have to interact with Your Word and to gain insight into all I need in order to become a better friend to all those You place in my path.

Supplication

God, make me a better friend. Make me the kind of friend people want to go to in order to gain insight and wisdom. Develop my spiritual maturity and my understanding of Your Word so I can be a reliable sounding board for those seeking Your will as they make choices in life.

I want to be known as a good friend to others. I want the reputation of being the kind of friend who consistently shares Your kingdom perspective in everything I say and do. Help me be all this much more in every relationship I have, whether at work, in the community, in my neighborhood, in the church, or in my family. Develop my skills so that I grow into what it means to be a friend reflective of those who are true kingdom heroes in Your view.

In Christ's name I pray, amen.

4

PRAYING FOR RELATIONAL COMMITMENT

Elijah said to Elisha, "Stay here please, for the LORD has sent me as far as Bethel." But Elisha said, "As the LORD lives and as you yourself live, I will not leave you." So they went down to Bethel.

2 KINGS 2:2

Adoration

God, You are faithful even when I am faithless. Your Word tells me this in 2 Timothy 2:13: "If we are faithless, He remains faithful, for He cannot deny Himself." But I have also experienced this. You faithfully stood by me and with me when others gave up on me. I felt Your presence when others left me alone. So because of this experience as well as the promises in Your Word, I know You will never leave me and You will never forsake me.

The level of Your relational commitment reaches higher than I can comprehend. This truth allows my heart to rest as I trust that You will always be there for me whenever I need You. You are one prayer away from a conversation. You are never too busy to share Your heart and Your time with me. I love You for this. I praise You for this. And I want to reflect Your love in the relationships I have as well.

Confession

God, I confess that I have not always remained relationally committed in every relationship I've had. Even when it comes to family or close relationships, I've thrown in the towel when conflict rose or other difficulties presented themselves. Sometimes I've felt inadequate to the situation, and rather than stand by feeling helpless, I've bowed out altogether.

Forgive me for failing to turn to You for strength and wisdom so that I could remain in difficult relationships in order to be there for the other person—like You are there for those who need You.

Thanksgiving

Heavenly Father, thank You that I can grow in my ability to be committed in my relationships, whether they are with family, friends, coworkers, neighbors, or people in any other relationship that have come my way. I'm not stuck. I can develop the ability to be more committed in challenging times.

Thank You for modeling what this looks like—what grace and kindness and unconditional love look like. Thank You for giving me relationships with others so I can experience life more fully through them. Thank You for opening up my heart and my mind to see how important relational commitment is, particularly with regard to revealing Your heart of love and compassion to others. I know a true kingdom hero does not abandon others, especially those in need. A true kingdom hero remains committed relationally throughout the trials of life.

Supplication

God, help me increase my level of loyalty and commitment to those who need me to step up to the plate and be there for them. Help me be present in my relationships with others. Help me show up. Help me be consistent. Give me wisdom on how important this is and how my presence can have a positive impact on other people. I want to be a kingdom hero who can be relied on to be there for those in my life when they need me the most.

In Jesus' name I pray, amen.

5

PRAYING FOR
DIRECTION IN VOCATION

*Let the favor of the Lord our God be upon us; and confirm for
us the work of our hands; yes, confirm the work of our hands.*

Psalm 90:17

Adoration

God, when You set out to create the earth and everything and
humanity populated on it in six days, You were clear about Your intentions and the work of Your hands. You brought about exactly what You
wanted, and then at the end of it all You said it was "good."

I adore You for Your ability to clearly define Your purpose and for
Your intentions in all You do. You don't waver. You aren't confused.
You know what You want and how to go about achieving it. I ask that You
receive my praise as I lift up Your name in giving You the glory due
You. Reveal more of Your creative intention so that I can learn from You.

Confession

God, at times I have hopped from interest to interest or focus to
focus, unsure where I should land. Sometimes I feel like I know what
my life is about and what I should be doing, but other times I feel lost.
I confess that I don't even always know what my calling is.

Forgive me for my lack of clarity and the frequency with which

I waver. In doing so, I waste time. I waste energy. Forgive me for the lack of diligence I have shown in pursuing the purpose You have for me, Lord.

Thanksgiving

Heavenly Father, thank You that I know I can look to You to find clarity in my calling and purpose. Thank You that I don't need to wander around aimlessly searching for what to do and what to focus on. You hold my purpose in Your hands as my creator.

Thank You that part of living as a kingdom hero comes about through fulfilling the purpose You have established for me. Thank You for this ability and the assurance that comes in knowing You will work all things out for good—no matter how they may look in the moment—if I will trust You and surrender to Your will for my life.

Supplication

God, give me great clarity for what I am to do for You and how I am to serve You in all that I do. Show me where I need to go like You told Abraham to set out and follow the path You had for him in a new land. Show me what I need to do. Place Your purpose in my heart like You placed the child in Sarah's womb. You are a God who fulfills purpose in those You call, so I'm looking to You to lead me according to Your kingdom plan for my life.

Make my path straight. Make me know Your ways just as You guided the Israelites through the wilderness so long ago. Help me not to get lost along the way or give in to fear in any way. Keep me on the straight and narrow path so I can live my life according to the greatness of Your kingdom calling for me.

In Christ's name I pray, amen.

6

PRAYING FOR BRAVERY

Be strong and courageous, do not be afraid or tremble
at them, for the LORD your God is the one who goes
with you. He will not fail you or forsake you.

DEUTERONOMY 31:6

Adoration

Holy God, Your strength and power and might never cower before
any opposition. You don't run in fear or hide when anyone rises up
against You. You are the model of what it means to be brave, fearless,
strong, powerful, and determined.

I praise You for the peace I feel knowing that Your bravery never fal-
ters or fails under pressure. I worship You because You are so strong that
I never have to fear if the enemy will defeat You. I honor Your might
and the way You display it through the construct of Your creation, and
I ask that You receive my worship and allow it to please You.

Confession

God, I confess that my bravery doesn't always show up when I want
it to. I admit that when I face difficulties and challenges or even opposition, fear raises its ugly head to stare me down and keep me stuck
in my tracks. My thoughts at times run wild with the many what-ifs
that can present themselves as potential threats to my safety, health, or
well-being.

Forgive me for my fears when they are rooted in self-preservation and dread rather than in a respect and an honor of You.

Thanksgiving

Father, thank You that I don't have to remain stuck where I am or at the lower level of bravery I seem to live with each day. Just because I may have missed the mark in the past doesn't mean I have to let that be my standard. I can grow stronger. I can live with greater displays of bravery like a kingdom hero should. I can remove fear from my conversations and thoughts and think and speak in a manner that pleases You.

Thank You for showing me the areas in my life where I need to improve in order to strengthen my ability to fulfill my calling as a kingdom hero in Your overall agenda and plan.

Supplication

God, please increase my bravery so that it removes all fear of that which I should not fear. The only fear I should have is a reverential fear of You. You reign and rule over all, and I ask that this truth be made manifest in all I think and do.

I ask to get rid of timidity. I ask You to help me remove debilitating shyness rooted in a low view of myself. I ask that You help me conquer pride and arrogance rooted in a fear of rejection. Show me how to live as a kingdom hero who consistently exhibits a compassionate and kind level of bravery so that others will know they can depend on me in times of difficulties and trials. Help me become known as a reliable kingdom disciple even in the middle of the mess and chaos of our culture.

In Jesus' name I pray, amen.

PRAYING FOR HONESTY

Lying lips are an abomination to the LORD, but
those who deal faithfully are His delight.

<small>PROVERBS 12:22</small>

Adoration

God, Your nature does not allow dishonesty within You. Lying and deception go against every fiber of Your being. You are holy. You are honest. You are truth. I worship You for Your honesty. I honor You for Your ability to remain truthful. I recognize Your unending commitment to what is real, righteous, and true.

Because of Your honesty, I can see what truth and reliability look like. I can make decisions based on the trustworthiness of Your Word. You are the true Kingdom Hero in every sense of those words because Your very essence embodies what it means to be honest and true.

Confession

Heavenly Father, I confess that I've not only told little white lies but also flat-out, full-on lies. Whether seeking to cover up difficulties I've faced, saying nothing was wrong in my life, or maneuvering around a challenging situation at work, I've caught myself in lies more often than I like to admit.

Forgive me for the many times I have lied. Forgive my dishonest heart that seeks the end above the means. Forgive my lack of faith in living as a kingdom hero committed to truth at all times.

Thanksgiving

God, thank You that Your power will protect me when I commit myself to living a life of truth. Thank You that You enable me to tell the truth when I lack the courage to do so myself. Thank You for the power of restraint and the grace of wisdom and clarity. Help me use both restraint and grace more often so I don't rush out and say things I will regret. Thank You that I can model to others what it means to grow in grace by sharpening my truth skills.

Supplication

God, I ask for open doors to practice telling the truth even when it makes me feel uncomfortable or puts me at risk for something I don't want to experience. Help me know, like the kingdom hero Daniel, that You will protect me in any "lions' den" if I stand up for truth and righteousness. Help me experience Your hand of deliverance in the little things so that my confidence will build to speak truthfully and honestly in the bigger things. Show me what it means to always be honest, even when being honest puts me in jeopardy.

May my words and the thoughts in my heart be pleasing to You as I seek to live my life according to the kingdom hero principles of honesty, integrity, truthfulness, and righteousness. I know that as I do, I will make myself more available for You to use me to make a kingdom impact on all those around me.

In Christ's name I pray, amen.

8

PRAYING FOR PERSONAL STRENGTH

Yet those who wait for the LORD will gain new strength;
they will mount up with wings like eagles, they will run
and not get tired, they will walk and not become weary.

ISAIAH 40:31

Adoration

God, You do not lack strength. You *are* strength. Your strength holds the world together. I praise You for showing me on a regular basis what true strength looks like. I worship You and adore You as I look to You as the strong God You are.

In Isaiah 63:5, Your Word says that only You are strong enough to bring about what You want and what we need. In that Scripture, You say through Your prophet, "I looked, and there was no one to help, and I was astonished and there was no one to uphold; so My own arm brought salvation to Me, and My wrath upheld Me." And just as it says in Isaiah 52:10, "The LORD has bared His holy arm in the sight of all the nations, that all the ends of the earth may see the salvation of our God."

Confession

Heavenly Father, forgive me for those times when I fail to ask You for strength. Forgive me when I instead rely on others for the strength You can so freely give me. I confess that I too often look to others to motivate me or strengthen me rather than turn to Your Word. Your Word provides me with peace and strength so easily and so quickly, and yet I still go somewhere else to seek both.

Please forgive me for doing this. And give me gentle nudges and reminders about where the source of all strength truly lies—within You and within the power of Your holy Word.

Thanksgiving

Lord, thank You for Your grace. Thank You for Your peace. Thank You for showing me how to grow in personal strength by modeling myself after You. Thank You for not throwing in the towel or even giving up on me when I give up on myself. Thank You that I can look to You and Your Word when I'm feeling frightened or weak and discover the strength I need to keep going.

I don't need to rush ahead without You. I can confidently wait for You and wait for Your direction as You undergird me with Your strength, Your wisdom, and Your guidance. Thank You for always being there for me, God, so that I know how to live my life as a kingdom hero who knows no limitations to spiritual and personal strength when rooted in You.

Supplication

God, make me into a kingdom hero more every day. Mold me into what brings You joy. Show me what it means to delight myself in You so that I will live in the strength You supply. You are my rock, and You are my fortress. I wait on You to give me all I need to rise up to the challenges that seek to overwhelm me.

As I look to You and Your hand to move in my life, I know I can trust You in every situation. Whether I am in ill health or experiencing adversity, my trust is strengthened as I look to You to be my guide. Show me the way I am to take, Lord, so that my life reflects the strength of who You are in all I do.

In Jesus' name I pray, amen.

9

PRAYING TO DEVELOP TENACITY

Blessed is a man who perseveres under trial; for once
he has been approved, he will receive the crown of life
which the Lord has promised to those who love Him.

JAMES 1:12

Adoration

God, I know perseverance and tenacity are hallmarks of a kingdom hero. Not throwing in the towel when difficulties arise or giving up when pressures come is part of living according to the image of Christ. I lift You up in praise as the life of Jesus models what it means to endure hardship, challenges, and even persecution while on earth yet remain tenacious about Your overarching will above all creation.

You are worthy to receive honor, glory, and adoration for the way You have remained steadfast throughout all eternity in the face of Satan's ongoing tactics, his trying to usurp Your rightful rule.

Confession

God, worry or a difficult reality surrounding me can slow me down or get me off track when I let them. But when I shift my focus from You to what seeks to consume me, I may actually lose spiritual ground.

Please forgive me for failing to remain tenacious in my pursuit of advancing Your kingdom agenda on earth. Forgive me for those times and even seasons when I have failed to be steadfast and consistent in the face of opposition. Forgive the weakness of my spirit when it should find its strength by abiding in You.

Thanksgiving

Heavenly Father, thank You for each new day. Thank You for every new opportunity to demonstrate my commitment to You and my faithfulness in following You. Thank You that, despite what comes against me, I can be tenacious in my spiritual walk because I can do all things through Jesus who gives me strength.

Thank You for the abundance of Your love and the empowerment of Your Spirit, which gives me the opportunity to go further in living out my destiny than I could ever go on my own. Thank You for demonstrating to me what true tenacity looks like through the life of Jesus Christ.

Supplication

God, give me the grace I need to live with a greater level of tenacity. Help me understand what spiritual tenacity truly is and how I can embody it in my daily life. Free me from the spirits of laziness and apathy. Loose that which binds me to the spirits of indulgence and self-pity. Show me a better way to spend my time than simply scrolling through social media feeds.

Lord, lift me up to live as a true kingdom hero who is steadfast about fulfilling Your plans for my life so that I can impact others with the love of Jesus Christ.

In Christ's name I pray, amen.

PRAYING FOR COURAGE

*Wait for the LORD; be strong and let your heart
take courage; yes, wait for the LORD.*

PSALM 27:14

Adoration

God, I know courage reflects a spirit of strength, and I know courage reveals a heart of consistent power and assurance. When someone acts in courage, we know they're not giving in to fear, doubt, or anxious thoughts.

Courage is lacking in so much of our world right now, but You have always exhibited courage in Your attributes and character. You are courageous, and You ask me to be courageous like You. You know what it's like to live with courage, and You know what courage is ultimately rooted in—a firm confidence in Your overarching sovereign rule and power. I adore You and worship You for Your attributes of strength, might, fortitude, and courage.

Confession

God, when courage slips away from me and I face the results of living in fear or doubt, I ask that You give me the freedom of Your forgiveness. Help me not to heap a feeling of condemnation or lack onto my already mounting fears. Show me what it means to fail but then get back up in the strength Your grace supplies.

I ask for Your guidance to show me the path to take that will give me opportunities to learn how to live with a greater level of courage. I want to be a kingdom hero, and I realize courage is one of the foundational attributes I need to do that.

Thanksgiving

God, thank You that my courage is not rooted in my own feelings or in my own abilities to accomplish things. My courage is firmly planted in Your power and Your sovereignty over all.

Thank You for patiently teaching me and guiding me toward living with greater courage every day. Much in this world seeks to cause fear. Yet when fear arises in my heart, I want to snuff it out with a faith that exhibits a kingdom-hero level of courage. Show me how to do that as I study Your Word and learn from You how to live my life with the attributes of a kingdom hero.

Supplication

God, I ask for greater courage. I ask for more experiences that will build and strengthen my courage muscles and increase my faith. I ask to see You more clearly and understand Your power more fully in my everyday life. I ask for faith that overcomes fear, and I ask for hope that defeats anxiety. I want to make decisions based on courage and compassion, not on self-preservation.

A true kingdom hero sets doubt aside when You call and when You guide. I ask that You enable me to live like that in every way so I can experience the fullness of the manifestation of Your will in my life.

In Jesus' name I pray, amen.

11

PRAYING TO INSPIRE OTHERS

*Anxiety in a man's heart weighs it down, but
a good word makes it glad.*

PROVERBS 12:25

Adoration

God, inspiration surrounds me every day. When I look at Your creation and the works of Your hands, my heart is lifted and my soul is stirred. I put my hope in You because You are the author and creator of all things. You cause the sun to rise, and You tell it where to set. You enable the trees to give life each spring. You bring forth the rain so that life is renewed from the long, dark winters of our days.

You are the inspiration for all I do and who I want to be as a kingdom hero in Your overall narrative on earth. I look to You to find my way and to understand what it means to live as a light of inspiration to those around me.

Confession

Lord, I want to use my life as a means of inspiring others around me. I want to bring an encouraging word into situations that lack life and joy. Forgive me for not being more intentional about using my time and the life You've given me to inspire others to have hope, embrace purpose, and pursue the passions You've placed within them. Forgive me for failing to lift those around me when and if I do.

I also ask that Your forgiveness release me from any guilt I feel and that I will walk into each new day with a fresh heart of joy so I can bring that joy into the lives of those I have the privilege of knowing on earth.

Thanksgiving

Father, thank You for Your inspiration in my life, which gives me the nudge to use my life to inspire others. Thank You for the inspiration I've received from reading Your Word and from studying the lives of kingdom heroes that show up in its pages.

Thank You for making me aware of the need to inspire others to stay strong in You and to follow You. Let me be an inspiration of faith on the job, in my home, in my community, and in my church. Let others see You in me as I model what it means to live as a kingdom hero every day and in every way.

Supplication

God, help my life to be an inspiration to many. Show me where I can inspire others and help them to become the greatest expression of themselves in Your love and care. I ask You to allow me to understand the power of inspiration on a larger level so I will take this role and attribute seriously.

Open doors for me to inspire others whether on social media or in the words I say when talking with them. Grow and develop this part of my life in such a way that other people look to me for encouragement and inspiration when they need something to lift them up. I ask for Your manifest presence in my life to shine through to those around me on a more consistent level.

In Christ's name I pray, amen.

PRAYING FOR GUIDANCE

I will instruct you and teach you in the way which you should go;
I will counsel you with My eye upon you.

PSALM 32:8

Adoration

God, Psalm 32:8 says You will teach me the way I should go. And in Isaiah 55:9, Your Word tells me Your ways are higher than my ways and Your thoughts are higher than my thoughts. Your wisdom outpaces my wisdom. Your will is perfect. I praise You for Your great insight and understanding on how things should be and how my life should take place to achieve the highest good for all involved.

I worship You for the depth of Your patience and the power of Your wisdom. You guide those who seek You like the stars in the sky guide travelers. You show the way I should go, directing my steps so that I accomplish the good You have determined for me to live out. You are the One who raises up kingdom heroes and emboldens them through Your personal guidance and direction. I lift up Your name in adoration and praise.

Confession

God, I confess to You that I often try to guide my own steps. I admit that I make my own plans and seek my own way. Even though

I know all wisdom comes from You and that You choose to freely give it to those who ask it from You, I often fail to ask for it. I often *forget* to ask for it. I often presume that my thoughts are somehow more strategic than Yours.

Forgive me for thinking too highly of myself and choosing not to tap into You as the source of all wisdom and direction. Forgive me for my personal failures and neglect of my relationship with You.

Thanksgiving

Thank You, God, for caring for me enough to give me multiple chances at getting this thing called life right. Thank You for showing me how to live, for guiding me where I need to go, and for giving me wisdom for the decisions I need to make.

Thank You for making Your wisdom available to me whenever I want it, whenever I ask for it, and whenever I choose to pursue a deeper, abiding relationship with You. Wisdom and guidance come to me simply by abiding in You. As I come to know Your heart and Your mind as revealed in the mind of Christ, I come to know the way I should go so that I live as a kingdom hero in my actions and the choices I make.

Supplication

God, I ask for wisdom. I ask for guidance. I ask that You direct my steps according to what will produce the greatest good for all mankind. Guide me in the way that will bring You the greatest glory and advance Your kingdom agenda on earth.

Help me know and see Your hand more clearly every day. Let Your guidance be on my lips and rest in my heart so that I'm innately attuned to Your will and Your way. I want to live as the kingdom hero You have created me to be. I want to please You by what I think, what I say, and what I do. Let Your Word be a light unto my path so that the steps I take are the best possible ones for the promotion of Your glory and the furtherance of Your will on earth.

In Jesus' name I pray, amen.

PRAYING FOR
A STRONG MORAL COMPASS

Woe to those who call evil good, and good evil; who
substitute darkness for light and light for darkness; who
substitute bitter for sweet and sweet for bitter!

Isaiah 5:20

Adoration

God, Your character is pure, peaceable, gentle, kind, holy, perfect, and without stain. Your attributes are rooted in a strong moral compass that clearly knows right from wrong. In a culture that doesn't make clear right from wrong, You are a refreshing source of purity and direction.

You light the way with Your morality—showing me what is truth, goodness, and righteousness. You make me know the way to take, which will always be the way of morality. I praise You and worship You for being a constant compass of morality in an ever-changing culture. I adore You for Your strength of character and Your consistency. Both allow me to see righteousness and avoid the confusion Satan seeks to produce in people worldwide through the changing of definitions, the altering of roles, and the labeling of light as darkness and darkness as light.

Confession

God, when my morality has slipped and I've stumbled into sin, You have always been there to forgive me and free me from both guilt and shame. Whether I have sinned in private or in public, You have never changed. And You never will. I'm confident that I can come before You no matter what I've done, and if I confess my sins, You are faithful and just to forgive me of them and cleanse me of all unrighteousness.

I admit that I have sinned more often than I have confessed. Please forgive me for any and all of my unconfessed sins so I can walk with my head held high in the freedom of Your great goodness and grace, comforted by the mercy You freely give me.

Thanksgiving

Father, thank You for setting the standard for me so that I can know and experience the fullness of Your love. Thank You for showing me what righteousness is and for calling me to live a life that is pleasing to You. Thank You for giving me something to aim for—and in so doing, for allowing me to live a life that will bring me good and bring glory to You.

I'm thankful for the high calling of being a kingdom hero; it will keep me from falling into the pit of the flesh as I keep my eyes focused on You and Your standard of morality for my life. Sometimes this culture will confuse me because it calls light the darkness and labels the darkness as light. Satan is the master deceiver, and I have fallen prey to his deception more often than I like to admit. But I thank You that Your truth rules over all. I thank You that You are the light shining in the distance to show me the way to take and to reveal to me what is truth in a world that constantly questions and mislabels truth.

Supplication

God, give me a strong moral compass and allow the Holy Spirit to convict me of sin so I will confess and repent and be forgiven. I want to walk as a kingdom hero according to the truth of Your righteousness. Help me discern truth from lies and discern morality from immorality. Put a barrier around me to keep Satan's deception from reaching my heart and my mind.

In Christ's name I pray, amen.

14

PRAYING FOR
RELATIONAL COMPETENCE

*Therefore I, the prisoner of the Lord, implore you to walk
in a manner worthy of the calling with which you have
been called, with all humility and gentleness, with patience,
showing tolerance for one another in love, being diligent
to preserve the unity of the Spirit in the bond of peace.*

EPHESIANS 4:1-3

Adoration

Dear God, so much goes into the components of a strong and healthy relationship. Character qualities such as humility, gentleness, patience, tolerance, love, and diligence toward unity as outlined in Ephesians 4:1-3 are just some of those components. You embody all of these and more. You are the perfection of what relational harmony and competence look like.

I worship Your name for Your strength of heart when it comes to relating to humanity, Your creation, in the midst of all of our flaws and challenges. You are worthy of the praise I give You—and You are worthy of so much more.

Confession

God, while I desire relational competence and relational health,

I don't always bring to the table the character qualities essential to achieving them. Show me what it means to truly repent so that I don't repeat my relational sins or patterns.

Where there is toxicity and I am the cause of it, convict me so that I can turn from it, seek healing internally, and discover how to relate to others in the manner of a kingdom hero. I want to serve You more, and I know relational health is one of the key components to doing that since love undergirds Your kingdom agenda in all ways.

Thanksgiving

God, thank You for the many relationships in my life that are strong and based on the kingdom principles of mutual honor, gentleness, humility, and love. Thank You for the role models You have placed in my life to guide and direct me toward a life of relational competence.

Thank You for giving me the high calling of being a role model for others as well. Show me how to do that more as I give You thanks in advance for providing those open doors to serve You as a kingdom hero.

Supplication

Lord, I ask You to bring people into my life who will teach me greater relational competence. I ask You to bring those whom I can teach as well. Help iron to truly sharpen iron. Let our words be full of grace, kindness, and humility. Keep judgment and critical spirits far from us. Let us esteem one another as higher than ourselves. In so doing, we will live as the kingdom heroes You have created us to be.

In Jesus' name I pray, amen.

15

PRAYING FOR DEVELOPED SKILLS AND TALENTS

There are many workmen with you, stonecutters and masons of stone and carpenters, and all men who are skillful in every kind of work. Of the gold, the silver and the bronze and the iron there is no limit. Arise and work, and may the LORD be with you.

1 Chronicles 22:15-16

Adoration

God, the creation of Your hands reflects Your multiplicity of skills. The way this world works and how everything is perfectly aligned—from the earth's atmosphere to its animals to our solar system—gives insight into the depth of Your knowledge and wisdom.

This knowledge and wisdom is made manifest in Your skills carried out in the earth. Without Your supreme skills, we would not be able to survive here. We would not have the perfect oxygen we need to breathe. We would fail to have the temperatures or rain or life that causes all things to work together. We wouldn't even have the ability to reproduce life apart from Your skill in how You made human beings.

I praise You for who You are above all and over all, and I praise You for how Your hands hold all things together.

Confession

God, I want to live as a kingdom hero who utilizes all the skills and talents You have placed within me. Yet I know I haven't fully realized some of them due to not sharpening them. In some cases, I'm not sure I've even identified them. Forgive me for any wasted time or wasted talents and skills.

Also, too often I've put aside a skill or talent that didn't seem to produce much to advance Your kingdom agenda. Forgive me for that. Show me what I need to do to walk in a greater level of awareness of how best to honor You with the work of my hands.

Thanksgiving

God, thank You for the way You have made me. Thank You for giving me so much opportunity to express my skills and talents for the glory of Your kingdom and the advancement of Your will on earth. Thank You for allowing me the freedom to explore my talents and skills in such a way that I can discover how they connect to my passions and hopes.

I want to live as a kingdom hero using my skills and talents in the best way possible. Over time You have directed so many people to do what You needed them to do. I want to be the same in Your kingdom. I want to be called on by You for an express purpose and plan.

Supplication

God, show me how I can sharpen my skills and talents. Help me also to identify ones I'm not yet aware of. Open my heart and my mind to explore new ways to serve in Your kingdom as the kingdom hero I was created to be. Help me become better at all the things You've gifted me to do as a kingdom hero.

In Christ's name I pray, amen.

16

PRAYING FOR SPIRITUAL STRENGTH

Be strong in the Lord and in the strength of His might.

EPHESIANS 6:10

Adoration

Father, I recognize my need to find my strength in You. I know the strength I have spiritually is rooted in Your Holy Spirit's presence in my life. I praise and worship You for giving me the ability to understand this truth. I worship You for Your strength of heart and Your willingness to strengthen me. I ask that You receive my praise and respond to it by giving me a greater sense of peace when I think about You or about what causes me fear or concern and worry.

Show me greater glimpses of You so that I will rest in You fully, according to the strength of Your might, not according to my own strength.

Confession

God, forgive me for too often trying to wage spiritual warfare in my own strength. When I do that, I fall short because my strength is no match for the enemy. Only in You do I find the spiritual strength I need to wage victorious spiritual warfare.

Show me how to recognize when I'm dipping into my own strength rather than into Yours so I can catch myself before I go too far only to face defeat. Thank You for Your great grace and forgiveness, which You have given me time and time again.

Thanksgiving

Thank You, Father, for allowing me to tap into Your spiritual strength in such a way that I can overcome the enemy and his schemes and strategies to defeat me. You are the strength I need to live a victorious spiritual life.

I thank You that I can be confident in living as a kingdom hero when I put on the full armor of God and live my life according to the principles of spiritual warfare as outlined in Your Word. Thank You for giving me Your Word so that I can study it and know what to do when opposition rises up against me. Show me how to use the weapons of spiritual strength in order to live as a kingdom hero according to Your purpose for my life.

Supplication

Father, I ask for Your patience to teach me how to wage victorious spiritual warfare against an enemy who seeks to overpower and deceive me. Walk with me on this path of life so that the steps I take are ones a kingdom hero would be grateful to look back on. I don't want to live with regret; I want to live in full faith and complete confidence, rooted and resting in You as my strength.

Embolden me to speak out against immorality and wrongdoing in our world. Give me courage to combat the enemy's schemes and conniving ways. Make me strong, Lord, in the strength of Your might.

In Jesus' name I pray, amen.

17

PRAYING FOR DEVELOPED SPIRITUAL GIFTS

Since we have gifts that differ according to the grace given
to us, each of us is to exercise them accordingly: if prophecy,
according to the proportion of his faith; if service, in his serving;
or he who teaches, in his teaching; or he who exhorts, in
his exhortation; he who gives, with liberality; he who leads,
with diligence; he who shows mercy, with cheerfulness.

ROMANS 12:6-8

Adoration

God, thank You for giving us spiritual gifts. Your creative ability is what allows each of us the opportunity to learn and grow in them. Because of the greatness of who You are, we can aim for and achieve greatness as kingdom heroes living underneath the overarching rule of Your kingdom agenda.

This world knows no limits to what You can do and what You can create. It doesn't contain You in any way. Rather, You are the One who sets the limits on creation and establishes gifts in us. The spiritual gifts you give are what make living out Your kingdom agenda on earth possible, and I praise You for this.

Confession

Father, I confess that I have often forfeited spiritual gifts You've given me simply due to a lack of use. I have lost out on opportunities to maximize my gifts because of a lack of interest in them or even a lack of awareness of them. But they have been given to me for a purpose. You have chosen my path, and You have a good plan for why I should pursue it.

Forgive me for the seasons in my life when my gifts have lain dormant.

Thanksgiving

Holy God, thank You for the mind You gave me. Thank You for providing me with a purpose through the use of gifts that can bring You glory and others good. Thank You for Your kindness in blessing me with the ability to do so many things well.

Thank You that I can still explore all that I can do to maximize my potential in Your kingdom. Thank You for awakening my heart and mind to know You more fully. Thank You that as I come to know You more fully, I will grow and develop the gifts You have placed within me.

Supplication

God, sharpen my gifts in such a way that serves You. When appropriate, show me how to set myself apart like Daniel did in Scripture so that others took notice of how well he did his job. I ask for Your wisdom and insight on how to develop my gifts in a way that honors You, brings good to others, and gives me satisfaction in carrying out the purpose for which I am here on earth.

Let me find joy in what I do as You bless my work in Your church on earth. Let me enjoy their use and live well in the spiritual life You have given me.

In Christ's name I pray, amen.

PRAYING FOR EMPATHY

Rejoice with those who rejoice, and weep with those who weep.

ROMANS 12:15

Adoration

God, You are a compassionate Lord. Your heart beats with the echoing sound of love and mercy. You embody what it means to know what others are going through because You came in the form of Jesus Christ so You could identify with what we feel and what we go through.

I worship You for caring so much and for Your willingness to become a man so You could rejoice with those who rejoice and weep with those who weep. You came to experience the emotions of our own limitations and to show us how much You care. I honor Your heart and Your love and Your mercy, all of which You have for all of humanity.

Confession

Father, I don't always rejoice with those who are rejoicing. In fact, many times I'm jealous of those who rejoice. I envy their lives. I confess this as a sin before You and ask for Your forgiveness for the coldness of my heart. It keeps me from celebrating someone else's victories as I should.

I also confess that I don't always weep with those who weep. Sometimes I'm indifferent to other people's pain. My heart has grown increasingly apathetic to the trials and difficulties other people face. Forgive me for the pride in my own heart that stops me from being more compassionate and caring toward others.

Thanksgiving

Thank You, God, that You have modeled what it means to care for others. You have shown us that we are to live with hearts that are honest, open, and full of love. Satan desires to turn our hearts to stone so we can't live out Your commandment that glorifies You the most— Your command to love.

Thank You for making me aware of the importance of love and caring so I can prioritize them. Thank You for giving me the ability to grow and develop this part of my life so I can reflect You more and more in all I say and do.

Supplication

Father, make my heart soft so I can feel for others as I should. Help me not to remain behind the pretense of pride but rather to fully empathize with others in the life situations they're struggling through.

I know love begins with letting go of my own wants and desires and placing the desires of others ahead of my own. I want to honor You with my heart, but way too often I get stuck seeking to honor myself. Show me what I need in order to grow in this area so I can love as You have called me to love. Show me what I need to do differently in order to fully embody this character quality of a kingdom hero.

In Jesus' name I pray, amen.

PRAYING FOR PURPOSEFUL SPEECH

Let no unwholesome word proceed from your mouth, but only
such a word as is good for edification according to the need
of the moment, so that it will give grace to those who hear.

EPHESIANS 4:29

Adoration

Holy God, Your words contain within them the very power of life itself. You formed the earth with just Your words. You spoke light into existence with just Your words. You made the ground on which we walk with just Your words. You fashioned the oceans. You created the animals. You spoke the whole universe into being.

Words are powerful. Words matter. Words can create, and they can also tear down. You use Your words intentionally and to produce life. I worship You for the power of who You are and the power of Your purposeful speech.

Confession

Father, I ask for Your forgiveness and Your mercy for the misuse of my speech throughout my life. I haven't always used my words wisely. Far too often I've complained or spoken about things I should not have even mentioned. Far too often I've ushered in my own defeat through my mouth and the things I've said.

Lord, forgive me for hurting others with my speech as well. Forgive me for what I've said to denigrate others made in Your image. Forgive me for allowing Satan to use my mouth as a tool to bring about evil rather than intentionally allowing You to use it as a tool to bring about good.

Thanksgiving

God, thank You for the power of my words. Thank You for opening my heart and my mind to understand how important it is to mean what I say and to say what I mean. Words have power. Words can cast a mountain into the sea, like Jesus said. Thank You for giving me the power of speech. My prayer is that my speech brings about good at all times and that I use it to build up both myself and others.

Thank You for giving me the opportunity to influence the world for good through what I say—whether it's what I say vocally, or what I post on social media, or even what I write in an email or a letter. Thank You for this great gift and power You have given me in order to bring about good.

Supplication

God, help me wisely use my words to bring about good and usher in greater days. Teach me to use them purposefully and in such a way that emphasizes faith and kingdom values. Help me shape the world around me in a positive way. And help me do this by what I say, post online, or share with others in some other way.

I want to be intentional about what I say so that I use my speech in productive and meaningful ways, both to help usher in a greater level of love and healing throughout our world and to allow a greater level of personal satisfaction and blessing in my own life.

In Christ's name I pray, amen.

20

PRAYING FOR A GREATER AWARENESS OF WHAT OTHERS FACE

When Jesus therefore saw her weeping, and the Jews who came with her also weeping, He was deeply moved in spirit and was troubled, and said, "Where have you laid him?" They said to Him, "Lord, come and see." Jesus wept.

JOHN 11:33-35

Adoration

I adore You, heavenly Father. One of the reasons I adore You so much is Your willingness to become acutely aware of what we face as humans on earth. You weren't content to just analyze us from afar. Rather, You came in the form of a man so You could feel and understand the grief that causes our tears. Through Jesus Christ You experienced our hurt and frustration. You felt our fears. You understood what it meant to weep because You also wept as Christ.

I worship You for Your ability to grieve as we grieve, just as you grieved with Lazarus's family as he lay dead. I worship You for Your ability to desire as we desire. I worship You for Your ability to feel, to know, and to experience all of life.

Confession

Father, it's easy to become so preoccupied with my own life that I forget to even care what others are facing or going through. Forgive me for those times and even prolonged periods when I'm so self-absorbed that I don't stop to take in what others are feeling.

Show me how to be more aware so that I don't continually miss the mark on this kingdom hero character quality. Forgive my lack of concern when humanity has to face and people have to deal with so many difficult challenges.

Thanksgiving

God, thank You for the ability to grow in my awareness of what other people are facing, especially through social media or other digital sources. You've allowed the world to be a much smaller place with information now traveling so quickly around the globe. Thank You that I can gain greater insights and understandings into the myriad issues facing people worldwide.

Thank You for helping all of us recognize the need for a larger amount of collective compassion toward one another. This comes through a greater awareness of what others face and what life is like for those outside of our own set of circumstances or background.

Supplication

Father, help me care more for others. Help me gain a better understanding of what other people face in their daily lives. Help me look beyond what I can see and understand so I get a glimpse into the struggles so many people deal with on a regular basis. Show me ways to develop relationships outside of my normal circles so I can expand my awareness and get to know people who aren't like me.

I also ask for the ability to refrain from judgment so that I can grow in my levels of compassion and empathy for those around me.

In Jesus' name I pray, amen.

21

PRAYING FOR THE SPIRITUAL GIFT OF MERCY

Blessed are the merciful, for they shall receive mercy.

MATTHEW 5:7

Adoration

God in heaven, thank You for Your mercy. I worship and praise You, for You are a merciful God. Your mercy gives me access into Your eternal kingdom. Your mercy sent Jesus to die on behalf of an entire world in sin. Your mercy shows me how to live each day filled with gratitude and praise.

Thank You for being full of mercy. Thank You for being slow to anger. If Your anger were not slowed, I would have lost my way so long ago. I would not have been given the opportunity to learn and grow and develop. Who is a God like You, a God who can show mercy like You do?

Confession

Father, mercy is a great gift when I receive it, but when I should give it to others, it's difficult to give. Yet I know a true kingdom hero lives with a merciful heart and a willingness to give mercy to those who need it most.

Forgive me for the times I've withheld mercy when given the opportunity to share it with others. Forgive me for failing to live as a kingdom hero when I choose not to demonstrate mercy through what I say or do. Forgive me for oftentimes holding others to a standard much higher than I have even set for myself.

Thanksgiving

Father, thank You for mercy. Thank You for the lessons that come from learning about mercy through experiencing it. I don't want to forget these lessons. I don't want to take mercy for granted. I want to live in a continual state of gratitude so I don't take the mercy given to me for granted. I know that when I do live in continual gratitude, I'll be able to show others mercy like I should.

Thank You for enlarging my heart and my awareness of love and mercy to such a degree that I can reflect kingdom hero principles in my life. Thank You for loving me enough that You want to see me grow and develop these qualities so I can reflect You more in who I am and what I do.

Supplication

Father, I ask for an increased level of the gift of spiritual mercy in my heart and in my thoughts. I ask for my thoughts to be free from judgment and pride. I ask that my thoughts start by giving others the benefit of the doubt and looking for ways to better understand what they're going through. I ask for open doors to extend mercy to those in need, whether through offering forgiveness, assistance, or in any other manner.

Show me how I can be a kingdom vessel of mercy to those around me. I want to be a light that lifts others to the place where they can seek You in a deeper and more meaningful way. Show me how to do that. Show me how to use the spiritual gift of mercy to help me do that even more than I ever thought possible. I ask for Your continued mercy to manifest itself in my life, Lord. And I also ask that You surround me with friends and family who will choose to give mercy rather than judgment when I do or say something wrong.

In Christ's name I pray, amen.

22

PRAYING FOR PERSONAL CONFIDENCE

*The LORD will be your confidence and will
keep your foot from being caught.*

PROVERBS 3:26

Adoration

Lord, I worship You for the strength of who You are. I can rest knowing You are at the helm. I can rest knowing You are in control. I can rest knowing You are the sovereign King who rules over all.

I worship You for who You are, the King of kings and Lord of lords. I honor You for who You are—the great, mighty God who reigns supreme. Receive my praise as I lift up Your name to honor You. Receive the worship of my heart as I seek to bring You glory through these prayers. May Your name be great over all this world. And may those who seek to know You find themselves in awe of You as they come to realize how powerful You truly are.

Confession

God, I'm tired of feeling so afraid. I'm tired of lacking personal confidence whether at work or in social relationships. I'm tired of lacking personal confidence when it comes to the decisions I must make or even when I consider my health. Worse, because I don't know always know what decision to make, I sometimes misplace my confidence. I put it in human wisdom rather than in the divine wisdom placed within me through Jesus Christ in me, as represented by the Holy Spirit.

I'm asking You to forgive me for that. I also ask for Your forgiveness for ignoring the truths spoken to me through the power of the Spirit. Forgive me for shifting my gaze from the greatness of who You are onto the uncertainties this life has to offer. When I do that, my confidence dwindles.

Thanksgiving

Thank You, God, that I can rely on You to deliver me when times are tough. Thank You that I can depend on You to guide me into the wisest choices to make. Thank You for boosting my confidence when I look to You, because I know You know the end from the beginning. You know what is about to transpire. You can direct me so that I take the right and necessary steps to live my life as a kingdom hero.

Thank You that all I need to do in order to increase my personal confidence is recognize that Christ lives in me and that He is the hope of glory. Within me dwells the perfection of the divine Holy Spirit, and I have full access to all wisdom through the gift of this relationship in me. Thank You for making it so simple to understand and so readily available to access.

Supplication

God, I ask that You remind me how to increase my personal confidence. Help me remain confident even when Satan seeks to plant doubts in my heart and mind. Show me what I need to do to keep my thoughts steadfast so that I don't waver in insecurity and fear.

Satan enjoys planting seeds of fear in my mind, but I resist those seeds in the name of Jesus Christ. In Christ, I am confident. I am secure. I am divinely guided and protected. I ask that You enable me to live out these truths in the spirit of being a true kingdom hero in all I do and say.

In Jesus' name I pray, amen.

23

PRAYING FOR CONFIDENCE IN GOD

*Not that we are adequate in ourselves to consider anything
as coming from ourselves, but our adequacy is from God.*

2 Corinthians 3:5

Adoration

Lord, You are wholly adequate. You are the sum total of all things, but You are also unique as one. Everything that exists, exists only because You exist. Only in You and through You do all things hold together. Without You the earth would be hurled from its rotation. Without You the stars would plummet from the sky. You are the supplier of all things and the source of all things because You are the creator of all things.

I praise and worship and adore You for the fullness that resides in You. I lift up Your name in praise for the power that is present in Your very being.

Confession

Father, I need to look to You more as the source for my own stability and calm. I need to remind myself that You are completely adequate to handle anything and everything I face.

Forgive me when I forget this truth and look to myself or to others in whom I put my trust. Forgive me for when I seek to walk according to my own wisdom, falling flat in the process. Please forgive me for trying to plan my own way and not holding my plans up for Your consideration. When I do that, I'm telling You I don't place confidence in You or in Your ability to instruct me on the ways I should go. Please forgive me for all of these failures.

Thanksgiving

Thank You, God, that You know all things. Thank You for saying You will give us insight into Your adequacy and all that You know if we will just ask for it. I can walk confidently throughout my life if I will just rest in a greater confidence placed in You.

Show me how to do this. Show me how to remain steadfast in my commitment to look to You and Your hand to guide me. Thank You that I can experience all that life has to offer—the abundant life—when I walk in the confidence of knowing who You are and that You are present in me at all times. Thank You that I'm growing and developing as a kingdom hero each day through my prayers.

Supplication

Father, show me how to live with a greater confidence in You as my Lord and King. Show me how to release fear and replace it with faith. I ask for Your strength to renew my strength when and where it is lacking. I ask for Your power to infuse me with supernatural power so I can boldly declare Your name in all I do.

Give me a renewed passion for knowing You, Lord. Also give me an increased desire to make Your name known throughout the peoples on this planet. Do Your work within my heart so I can carry out the purpose and plan You have for my life in Your kingdom agenda.

In Christ's name I pray, amen.

24

PRAYING FOR THE ABILITY TO FORGIVE

Bearing with one another, and forgiving each
other, whoever has a complaint against anyone; just
as the Lord forgave you, so also should you.

COLOSSIANS 3:13

Adoration

Father, forgiveness is critical for me to experience a close, intimate relationship with You. I need Your forgiveness for my sins and preoccupations that seek to usurp Your rightful place in my mind and heart.

I worship You because You are able to forgive where most could not. I praise You because You extend forgiveness like the water rushing down a stream, so easily and smoothly. I lift up Your name in praise knowing that only You can forgive at the level You do. No one else even comes close. Your ability to forgive those who have hurt You, who have rejected You, who have dismissed You and more is beyond my comprehension. But I give You praise for what I do know and understand, and I honor Your name, for You are worthy of all honor.

Confession

God, the ability to forgive is harder than I like to admit. It's easy to say I'll forgive someone, but when it comes time to either talk to that person or talk about that person with others, my actions and words can wind up less than heroic. That's when I realize I never actually forgave them. Instead, I carry around resentment that should have been released with forgiveness.

Father, forgive me for my lack of forgiveness toward others. Forgive me the hardness of my heart and for choosing to hold others to a higher standard than the one I want You to hold me to. Forgive me for failing to extend forgiveness when I have received it so often from You.

Thanksgiving

Thank You, Lord, for showing me what it means to forgive and forget through how You treat me. Thank You for allowing me to experience the freedom that comes through experiencing forgiveness firsthand. Thank You for giving me the strength and spiritual maturity to forgive others as well—if I choose to do so. I want to forgive, and that's why I rely on Your strength to enable me to do so.

Thank You that I'm not walking this path alone. Thank You that I can depend on You for difficult things, like extending forgiveness to someone who has truly hurt me. Thank You for the power of love. That power can help me overcome any hesitancies I have toward forgiving someone who has hurt me or continues to hurt me, as well as toward anyone who has hurt or continues to hurt someone I love.

Supplication

Lord, increase my ability to forgive others. Do what needs to be done in order for my heart to grant forgiveness to others instead of choosing to hold on to bitterness. The resentment I cling to harms me, not the people who hurt me. I want to live as a kingdom hero lives—through releasing the debts of others when they have sinned against me or against someone I love.

Show me what I need to do to forgive quickly and not allow pain or bitterness to build and expand. Please help me reflect Your image as a kingdom follower of Jesus Christ through the way I extend forgiveness.

In Jesus' name I pray, amen.

25

PRAYING FOR THE ABILITY TO APOLOGIZE

If you are presenting your offering at the altar, and there remember that your brother has something against you, leave your offering there before the altar and go; first be reconciled to your brother, and then come and present your offering.

MATTHEW 5:23-24

Adoration

Heavenly Father, You are perfect and righteous, so You have never needed to apologize. You don't know what it is to grieve someone because of a sin You committed against them. You have never experienced regret immediately after hurting someone with Your unkind words or actions because You are always kind.

But You do know humanity regularly wrestles with offending one another and the need to reconcile. I praise You and worship You for loving us enough to show us how to do that. I worship You for allowing us to witness the testimony of Jesus Christ, who reconciled the lost world to a living God through His death and resurrection. May Your name and the name of Jesus Christ be exalted above all else.

Confession

God, I confess that I don't always admit to others what I've done to hurt them and apologize. That requires a mindset and heart of humility, and sometimes I find that humility difficult.

Forgive me for my pride. Forgive me for my self-righteousness or high view of myself that keeps me from apologizing to those I've wounded through my words or actions. Cleanse me from the unrighteousness of self-righteousness so I can experience the pureness of love abiding in me.

Thanksgiving

Thank You, God, for reminding all of us in Matthew 5 to first be reconciled to one another as brothers and sisters in Christ before we present our offerings to You. Thank You for pointing out the critical nature of asking for forgiveness. Thank You for emphasizing the importance of right relationships with one another built on a foundation of honesty, humility, grace, and forgiveness.

The gift of Your forgiveness has transformed my life in so many ways. I want to be an extension of Your forgiveness to others, and I also want to help others forgive me by apologizing when I need to and it's the right thing to do.

Supplication

Father, I want You to accept the worship and the offering I bring to You, but You say I first need to be reconciled with those I have offended. Emphasize this to me through tangible ways so I take this principle in Your Word seriously. I don't want to hold myself back from living as a kingdom hero in any way.

Enable me to grow and mature in such a way that apologizing when I'm wrong seems like the natural thing to do. Give me the courage to go to those I've hurt or offended in some way and apologize. Strengthen my resolve. Even if they're not asking me to apologize, remind me of the importance of doing so based on Your Word.

In Christ's name I pray, amen.

26

PRAYING FOR TOOLS TO OVERCOME ANXIETY

Be anxious for nothing, but in everything by prayer and
supplication with thanksgiving let your requests be made known
to God. And the peace of God, which surpasses all comprehension,
will guard your hearts and your minds in Christ Jesus.

PHILIPPIANS 4:6-7

Adoration

Father, I praise Your name and lift it up in adoration. I delight in bringing You praises because You are worthy to receive them all. You are confident. You are complete. You are strong. You are mighty. You are majestic. When I think of You, I don't think of an anxious, depressed God who doesn't know what to do. I think of the King of kings, the One who knows all things and is sovereign over all things.

Your power gives me peace. Your strength brings me ease. Your might makes me calm. I worship You for the gift of knowing You and resting in Your loving care under Your strong arm.

Confession

Holy God, anxiety can appear without warning. It can creep in through a post I read on social media, through a news headline I see, through hearing something potentially disturbing from friends, or even through just a thought in my own head. Anxiety can come so quickly that I don't always remember what to do when it does.

Forgive me for those times when I'm at a loss for knowing what to do and then try to resolve my anxious thoughts on my own. Forgive me for worrying rather than casting my cares on You. I know how much You care for me.

Thanksgiving

Lord, thank You for Your ability to see me through any difficulty, challenge, or storm. Thank You for Your willingness to comfort me through my fears and to calm my anxious thoughts. Thank You that my peace is only a prayer away. I can live as a kingdom hero, secure in my faith, because You are the source of my hope. You are the provider of my stability.

Thank You that I don't need to fear or worry when I don't know the outcome of what lies ahead of me. Thank You that I can rest knowing You feed the birds and yet You care so much more for me. I know You will always care for me.

Supplication

Heavenly Father, calm my heart and soften the thoughts of worry and anxiety that run through my head. Slow down those thoughts so I can find rest for my soul. I ask for an increased level of faith so that anxiety is no longer an option for my emotions.

I want to live as a kingdom hero who understands Your sovereign hand and what it means for me. I don't want to be tossed about like waves on a shore but rather live peacefully in the presence of Your love. Show me how, as Paul shared in 2 Corinthians 10:5, to take my thoughts "captive to the obedience of Christ." Show me how to let go of or remove any thoughts that don't align with Jesus or with Your kingdom agenda and its manifestation in my life.

In Jesus' name I pray, amen.

27

PRAYING FOR AN INCREASED ABILITY TO CARE

*Do not merely look out for your own personal
interests, but also for the interests of others.*

PHILIPPIANS 2:4

Adoration

Father, thank You for not merely looking out for Your interests but also for the interests of all of humanity. Thank You for not just making sure You had everything You needed but also making sure Your creation had everything it needed as well. If You hadn't, we wouldn't be here. We wouldn't be able to survive.

And because of the depth of Your care, I have all I need to live my life as a kingdom hero. You have shown care not only for my physical needs but also for my emotional needs and my spiritual growth. You are worthy of all praise, and I give You honor for the great levels of Your awesome care.

Confession

Heavenly Lord, I confess that my caring for others isn't where it needs to be. I confess that I naturally think of myself and my own needs before considering what other people need. My interests supersede the interests of those around me, and this is contrary to Your call for love.

Forgive me for my selfishness. Selfishness is not a trait of a kingdom hero. Forgive me for my apathy. Apathy is also not a trait of a kingdom hero. Allow Your forgiveness to cleanse me in such a way that the gratitude I have for it overflows into a greater depth and level of care for others.

Thanksgiving

Father, thank You for the opportunity to care for others. Thank You for not creating us to live in isolation but for Your purposes of community and relationship. Thank You for the love I experience in the relationships I have.

I want to be more caring so that the interests of others supersede my own. I want to fully live as a kingdom hero so that the world is impacted for good and for Your greater glory by the things I do and say. Thank You for reminding me of this important principle and character quality through Your Word found in Philippians 2:4.

Supplication

God, help me care for others at a higher level. Help me look to the interests of others more fully. Help me identify what other people may actually need in order to experience the fullness of their growth as believers in Jesus Christ. In this way, I'll be able to seek to meet those needs in ways You have gifted me to do.

Show me what I need to do in order to be better at this aspect of the Christian life. And when I do set out to meet the needs of others, please make it known to them that I do so out of my love and gratitude for all You have done for me and given to me.

In Christ's name I pray, amen.

28

PRAYING FOR THE WILL TO LIVE UP TO MY POTENTIAL

It is God who is at work in you, both to will and to work for His good pleasure.

PHILIPPIANS 2:13

Adoration

Father, You have set the standard of living up to our potential high. You have given so many examples of kingdom heroes in Scripture, and in doing so You have let me know what You desire of me. You want me to live up to the potential You have placed within me. You want me to honor You through my choices and what I do. I praise You and worship You for Your interest in me, and my potential motivates me to want to please You.

Thank You for caring so much for me that I feel Your care. It helps me want to honor You in all that I do so that my life itself is the worship and praise I give You.

Confession

Father, I confess that I don't always live up to my potential. Whether with what I say or what I do, I know I can do far better. Forgive me for wasting the potential You have placed within me. I want to maximize the gifts and talents You gave me. Forgive me for not prioritizing this more.

I confess that I sometimes even doubt my potential. I know this is actually doubting and questioning You, both because You made me in Your image and because Your Word tells me that nothing is impossible for me when I live a life of faith as a kingdom hero. Forgive me for doubting You, Lord.

Thanksgiving

Holy God, thank You for setting the bar high so I can aim at something meaningful. Thank You for showing me through Your Word that there's nothing I can't do if it is in Your will. You are the One in me, driving me to both will and work for Your good pleasure.

Thank You for taking part in this life journey with me so I'm not walking alone. Thank You for prompting me to do more with the gifts and talents You have placed under my kingdom stewardship. Thank You for the opportunities and open doors You have given me.

Supplication

Lord, help me seize every moment in such a way that allows me to maximize the potential You have given me. Show me what I need to do in order to demonstrate my full understanding of the calling You have placed on my life. I want to know You on a deeper level. And when I do come to know You more fully, I believe I will also expand my personal potential because it's tied directly to You. You are in me, both to will and to work for Your good pleasure.

Unleash Your good pleasure both in and through me, God, so that I can optimize the opportunities before me to live as a kingdom hero. Show me how to honor You through my choices and my words, and give me wisdom and insight on what I can do to improve my skills, talents, and gifts so I can get better at the purpose You have for me to live out.

   In Jesus' name I pray, amen.

29

PRAYING FOR DEEPER FAITH

Faith comes from hearing, and hearing by the word of Christ.

ROMANS 10:17

Adoration

Holy God, You don't need faith because You are the source of faith. You already know all there is to know about faith. I worship You and lift Your name in praise because of the greatness of who You are. You are sovereign, and You rule over all.

I recognize Your holiness and the truth that You embody. All truth is found in You. All faith is rooted in You. All hope is in You. All love comes from You. I honor You for who You are because You are the totality of faith, hope, and love. You are the manifestation of each of these. You reflect them to me and challenge me to live at a higher level in all of them. But You especially challenge me to grow and deepen my own personal level of faith.

Confession

Holy God, I confess that I don't have the level of faith I would like to have. I confess that I can't always rely on myself to muster up faith when I need it most.

Forgive me for my low level of faith despite my high aspirations to live as a kingdom hero when things get tough. Forgive me for focusing on what I can see with my eyes rather than on what I trust in my heart regarding Your Word and Your truth. Forgive my unbelief, Lord, and help me overcome it so that I honor You with a life full of faith in who You are and in what You say.

Thanksgiving

Lord, thank You for giving me Your holy Word. Thank You for allowing me to deepen my faith through listening to Your Word, through reading Your Word, or even through hearing the testimonies of other believers and seeing how they've followed You in faith. Thank You for surrounding me with such a great cloud of witnesses that I have more than enough examples for what it means to live out a heroic level of kingdom faith.

Thank You, Lord, for the depth of Your love, which extends itself to me through Your Word. I find wisdom in Your Word. I find guidance in Your Word. I find hope in Your Word. And my faith grows through the study, meditation, understanding, and application of Your Word.

Supplication

Father, grow my faith. Deepen my faith walk. Give me opportunities to take risks of faith so that I can learn for myself how faithful You are. I have heard the stories of those who lived with kingdom faith. But I want to experience these types of stories in my own life. I want to know what it's like to live with so much faith that I see Your hand show up in my life to overcome the enemy and the opposition that seeks to bring me down.

I want to advance Your kingdom agenda on earth, but I need great faith to do that. I ask for this great faith. I ask for it as a gift of Your favor in my life. And I ask that You continue to strengthen my faith muscles each day so I'm always growing.

In Christ's name I pray, amen.

30

PRAYING FOR EXPERIENCES THAT WILL GROW MY FAITH

The apostles said to the Lord, "Increase our faith!"

LUKE 17:5

Adoration

Holy God, You have always known what it's like to live in a con-stant state of belief. You have never needed Your faith increased or Your belief strengthened. You know what is true and how all things are held together by You. You understand the world in which we live. You also understand everyone's purpose. You have never suffered from a crisis of faith because You are the source of faith itself.

I honor and worship You for Your stability in the midst of such an unstable world. I lift up Your name in praise as I think on the calm-ness of who You are. This calmness rests in the assurance You have of knowing everything. Yet You make this calmness available to anyone who seeks You and desires to develop an intimate relationship with You through faith.

Confession

Father, I confess that I complain about my lack of faith far more often than I ask You to increase it. I doubt situations in my life or how

You will come through far more frequently than I go to You to resolve a situation. Prayer seems like an easy thing to do, and yet I don't pray as much as I should.

I know prayer doesn't have to be elaborate or long. The disciples prayed just three words: "Increase our faith." They were straightforward about what they wanted You to do. Forgive me for making my conversations with You in prayer at times more rote or difficult than they need to be. Help me go to You in prayer as easily as You have made it possible.

Thanksgiving

Lord, thank You that life is an ongoing learning experience. You don't cancel my opportunities to learn just because I don't get it right the first time. You are patient, and You allow for more opportunities to test my faith and for me to grow as a kingdom disciple. Thank You for increasing my faith.

I'm thanking You in advance, in faith, for this answer to my prayer. I want to live as a kingdom hero with great faith. I know You are going to honor my prayer because growing my faith is in alignment with Your will for my life. Thank You that I can pray with confidence, knowing You hear me and that You are able to bring about the fulfillment of my heart's desire through this prayer.

Supplication

Loving God, increase my faith. Increase the opportunities for it to be tested and mature. Show me what I can intentionally do to grow my faith at a greater level than ever before. Show me Your will for my life so I can step out in faith more fully than I ever have.

Will You also give me confidence boosters along the way? Give me stones of remembrance that I can set up in my heart and in my mind that will remind me of Your great faithfulness? I ask for these so that I don't lose heart or lessen my faith when I need it the most. You are able to bring me to a deeper level of faith so I can be an example to those around me, showing them what a kingdom hero living in today's contemporary culture looks like.

In Jesus' name I pray, amen.

31

PRAYING FOR OPPORTUNITIES TO WITNESS GOD'S POWER

The LORD said, "Behold, there is a place by Me, and you shall stand there on the rock; and it will come about, while My glory is passing by, that I will put you in the cleft of the rock and cover you with My hand until I have passed by. Then I will take My hand away and you shall see My back, but My face shall not be seen."

EXODUS 33:21-23

Adoration

Lord, Your power is great. Your glory is beyond what I can even witness without it affecting me. Moses wanted to see Your glory, but You would not allow Him to see the fullness of Your glory because in his humanity he would not be able to handle it. You said he would die. So You placed him in the cleft of the rock and covered him with Your hand. Then when You passed by, You allowed him to see Your back.

This is how powerful You are. We aren't even able to witness You in all of Your power because it would be more than we can handle. I praise You and worship Your name, for Your power is beyond my comprehension.

Confession

Father, I want to experience and witness Your power, but I confess that I oftentimes get so preoccupied with what I'm doing in my life that I forget to even look for Your power.

Forgive me for how busy I allow myself to be and how little time I spend focusing on my relationship with You. Forgive me for failing to pause and take notice of how great and powerful You are. You have revealed Your power through Your creation, yet I often pass by even humanity, made in Your image, with disinterest. Please forgive me for this.

Thanksgiving

Holy God, thank You for allowing Moses to experience a glimpse of Your glory and power. Through his experience, I've learned that You will allow me to experience a glimpse as well. Whatever You know I can handle, You will allow me to have. I ask for this, and I thank You for hearing my prayer and responding. Thank You that I can pray to You with full confidence in Your ability and willingness to respond.

Supplication

God, please give me more opportunities to experience Your power. Give me occasions when I can see and identify Your moving within them. Show me what it means to live as a kingdom hero who recognizes Your fingerprints on my life experiences. Help me identify Your engagement and power. Help me not attribute Your power and glory to anyone else or to myself. Rather, give me discernment as a kingdom hero to recognize and enjoy the display of Your power and glory in my life.

In Christ's name I pray, amen.

32

PRAYING FOR STRENGTH DURING STRUGGLES

God is our refuge and strength, a very present help in trouble.
Therefore we will not fear, though the earth should change and
though the mountains slip into the heart of the sea; though its
waters roar and foam, though the mountains quake at its swelling
pride. There is a river whose streams make glad the city of God, the
holy dwelling places of the Most High. God is in the midst of her,
she will not be moved; God will help her when morning dawns.

PSALM 46:1-6

Adoration

God, You are my refuge and my strength. You are a very present help in times of trouble. I will not fear when You are near. Even if things change on this earth, even if the culture becomes difficult to understand or navigate at times, I will look to You as my strength and shield. You are in the midst of Your creation. You have set the stars in their places. You have created the oceans and told them where to stop. You cause the rain to water the ground and provide life to the planet and all the people on it.

You are the source of all strength because You are strength.

Confession

Lord, I should know better by now, but I still depend on my

strength rather than on Yours when times get tough. I need to look to You more. In You is where I find the source of my strength. When I am weak, You perfect strength within me because that's when I realize I have to look to You.

I ask for Your power and strength to be present in my life. But more than that, I ask for Your mercy and forgiveness for forgetting to turn to You in my greatest times of need or even in the daily difficulties that arise.

Thanksgiving

Thank You, God, for Your willingness to strengthen me during times of challenge and trouble. Thank You for showing me how to pray to You in such a way that expresses what I truly need most. Thank You for helping me understand the difference between relying on my own strength and depending on You. Your Holy Spirit strengthens me when I let go of my own need for control. Thank You for the gift of the Holy Spirit within me through the sacrifice of Jesus Christ.

Supplication

Holy God, please give me strength to face the challenges in my life and in our culture. Give me strength to not cave into feelings of fear, dread, or worry about the future. Give me strength of character, strength of mind, and a strong hope. I ask for the strength to stay diligent in the work You have called me to do, and I ask that I won't become lazy. I also ask for the strength I need to witness to others about the saving power of Jesus Christ.

I need Your strength for so many things in order to live my life as a kingdom hero.

In Jesus' name I pray, amen.

33

PRAYING FOR PEACE FOR OUR PLANET

Glory to God in the highest, and on earth peace among men with whom He is pleased.

LUKE 2:14

Adoration

Father, thank You for sending Jesus Christ to earth so that peace can be provided. Thank You that the angels declared He would bring peace among men with whom You are pleased. I praise You, for You are the source of peace when all else looks chaotic and confusing.

You hold the earth together so that it functions in peace. You usher peace into our hearts when Your followers pray and ask for peace. I worship You for the peace You embody and are willing to display in Your creation, as well as to give to those who find favor with You.

Confession

Lord, it's easy to complain about the chaos in our country rather than to look to You for peace. It's easy to point fingers at those we think cause the chaos rather than to point people to You, the One who can usher in peace.

Forgive me for spending far too much time blaming the situations of chaos or those I think are causing them rather than focusing on peace and asking You to shower it onto our land. Forgive me for forgetting the solution to the situations that seem so out of hand—and also for failing to share that solution with others.

Thanksgiving

Heavenly Father, thank You that You can bring peace into places that seem so out of control. Thank You that Jesus could calm the waves just by telling them to be still. It doesn't take long for You to speak peace into a scene and have that scene change. You can even speak the word *peace* into my soul and calm my anxious thoughts. Thank You for showing me what I need to do to access Your peace through finding Your favor.

The angels said there would be peace among men with whom You are pleased. Thank You for giving me insight into how to live a life of peace.

Supplication

Holy God, I pray for peace for our planet. I ask that You replace all the anger, hurt, and resentment with peace and love. I pray that people will come to know how to love one another more fully, accept one another more graciously, and honor one another's presence. Help all of us be ambassadors of Your peace as we seek to live as kingdom heroes.

I pray for peace for those who lead us in our nations and for peace between nations. Heal the hearts that need to be healed. Mend the brokenness and heal the trauma. Encourage humanity to seek peace above all—and to also seek authentic, kingdom-based love.

In Christ's name I pray, amen.

34

PRAYING FOR KINGDOM VALUES

The fruit of the Spirit is love, joy, peace, patience, kindness, goodness, faithfulness, gentleness, self-control; against such things there is no law.

Adoration

Father, I lift up Your name in praise and worship as in You I see all of the kingdom values a kingdom hero needs. You are love, joy, peace, patience, kindness, goodness, faithfulness, gentleness, self-control, and so many other attributes. They all describe who You are. You are all of these perfectly, and I praise You for Your goodness and grace.

Your attributes are the model and standard for all of us as Your followers to use as a guide to make our personal decisions. You show us how to rein in our emotions and use the gift of emotion for good. I praise You because You are a loving Father who only wants to see each of Your children flourish with the right heart and spirit and in truth.

Confession

God, I would like to say that I always embody the kingdom values that make for a kingdom hero, but too often I do not. Forgive me for impatience. Forgive me when I doubt. Forgive me when I say harsh things or think harsh thoughts about others. Forgive my lack of self-control, which then leads me to indulge in ways or in things I should not. Forgive me when I allow anxious thoughts to strangle any ounce of peace You have placed in me.

I ask for Your forgiveness for all of this and more as I seek to align my life after Your attributes and in alignment with Your kingdom values.

Thanksgiving

Thank You, God, for outlining so many of Your kingdom values in Scripture so that no one has to guess what it means to live in a way that honors and glorifies You.

Thank You also for gifting me with the presence of the Holy Spirit so I have access to all I need to live with the full manifestation of the kingdom values in my life. Thank You for convicting me when I stray or do wrong so I can learn from my mistakes and sins and grow and mature into a kingdom hero. Thank You for reminding me that being a kingdom hero isn't only about what I do but also about who I am inside.

Supplication

Heavenly Lord, fill me with the Spirit to such a degree that I'm also filled with the fruit of the Spirit and live as a representative of Your kingdom. Your kingdom values are needed in our culture, communities, and churches. I want to be a light that helps others see the need for personal values and character qualities that reflect You. Where there is anger and hate, let me be a reminder of love. Where there is fear, let me model true confidence and patience.

Show me how to honor You as I embody the kingdom values You desire me to have. Show me how to reflect Your image to a world in need.

In Jesus' name I pray, amen.

35

PRAYING FOR OPEN DOORS TO SERVE

We are His workmanship, created in Christ Jesus for good works,
which God prepared beforehand so that we would walk in them.

EPHESIANS 2:10

Adoration

Father, You have created each of us with a specific purpose in mind. We are all Your workmanship, created in Christ Jesus to carry out good works that will advance Your kingdom agenda on earth. You have even gone ahead to prepare these good works so we can walk in them. You've established the paths. You've positioned the people. You've imbedded the skills and interests we need to help us on our way.

God, I praise You for how You orchestrate all things so holistically in order to bring about Your overarching plan.

Confession

Heavenly Lord, even though I am Your workmanship, created in Christ Jesus for good works, I don't always walk according to the plans You have for me. I even don't always notice the open doors You provide for me to serve You.

Forgive me for at times being so internally focused that I lose track of Your master plan. Forgive me for allowing distractions to keep me from identifying Your direction in my life. Cleanse me from the sins of pride, apathy, and independence so I can be ready to walk through the open doors You give me to help advance Your kingdom agenda on earth.

Thanksgiving

God, thank You for caring for me and creating me with a purpose in mind. Thank You for placing me here on earth for a reason and for giving me meaning. I am a kingdom hero when I walk according to Your plans for my life because You desire that I live heroically, based on the calling You have for me.

Thank You for inspiring my heart to pursue You more closely through guided prayers. Thank You for giving me open doors that I can walk through in order to experience more of Your plans and the meaning You have for me. I want to make a positive impact on the world around me, whether through what I think, say, or do. Lord, help me do that with a grateful heart, always remembering that all things come from You and are ordained by Your hand.

Supplication

Father, show me where You have opened doors for me to walk through so I can have a greater impact on the lives that surround me. Open my eyes to see and recognize Your leading in my life. Help me not shy away from opportunities to serve You but rather move forward with boldness and joy.

I ask for Your hand to guide me each step of the way. I ask that You expand the level of influence I have on those around me. I want to make a difference for good in the world. I want to be the kind of person who leaves a legacy of kingdom living so that others can learn from me and benefit by their interactions with me. Show me ways I can do that more each day.

In Christ's name I pray, amen.

36

PRAYING FOR FAITHFULNESS

He who is faithful in a very little thing is faithful also in much;
and he who is unrighteous in a very little thing is unrighteous
also in much. Therefore if you have not been faithful in the
use of unrighteous wealth, who will entrust the true riches to
you? And if you have not been faithful in the use of that which
is another's, who will give you that which is your own?

LUKE 16:10-12

Adoration

Father, faithfulness is the hallmark of a kingdom hero. Without faith and faithfulness, the natural result is that it's impossible to please You. This is because You are faithful. You are truth. You are holy. You are dependable. You know that for each of us to live as a kingdom hero, we need to take You seriously and rely on You much more than we tend to.

I worship and praise You because of Your great and holy name. I honor You in all that You do to demonstrate faithfulness in Your creation and to Your people. I love You, Lord, and I want my life to model You as much as it possibly can.

Confession

Heavenly Lord, I confess that I'm not always faithful. In fact, when challenges arise, I can slow down my spiritual progress as I seek to protect myself from potential dangers ahead.

Forgive me for my lack of faithfulness to kingdom values and to advancing Your kingdom agenda on earth. Forgive me for buckling under the weight of issues in my life. Forgive me for growing weary and wanting to take a break from the kingdom life and all it entails. I ask for Your cleansing love and grace to wash me fresh and give me a renewed energy to strive for a life of faithfulness.

Thanksgiving

God, thank You for the reward of faithfulness. In Your Word you say if I'm faithful in "a very little thing," I will also be faithful in much. You watch what I do with what You have given me, and You choose whether to give me more based on my own levels of faithfulness.

Thank You for giving me opportunities to demonstrate faithfulness in all that I do. Thank You for reminding me that a lot of what I receive in this life has to do with my own choices and how I decide to use the resources You give me.

Supplication

Holy Father, I want to be more faithful as I seek to live my life as a kingdom hero. I want to remain faithful to You and Your calling on my life so that I don't waver when difficulties arise. I want You to be happy with what You see me doing each day and how You witness me stewarding all that You have placed under my care to manage.

I ask for greater faithfulness to show up in my thoughts and to displace thoughts of weariness or doubt. I ask for greater personal conviction on the importance of living a life of kingdom faithfulness as Your follower.

In Jesus' name I pray, amen.

37

PRAYING FOR A POSITIVE MINDSET

Whatever is true, whatever is honorable, whatever is
right, whatever is pure, whatever is lovely, whatever
is of good repute, if there is any excellence and if
anything worthy of praise, dwell on these things.

PHILIPPIANS 4:8

Adoration

Father, there is so much negativity in the world. It surrounds us on all corners, revealing the undercurrent of Satan's ploys and schemes. Satan seeks to destroy all of the good You have created.

But he can't destroy it all because You are good and You have created a way for good to flourish when people follow You according to Your principles. One of Your kingdom hero principles is to manage our thought life according to Your values. Your values reflect truth, honor, righteousness, purity, excellence, and all things that are good. These are what describe You in the fullness of Your glory, and because of that I lift up Your name in praise.

Confession

Holy Lord, when I'm surrounded by negativity—whether through what people say in my relationships, or through what I hear on the news, or through what I read online—it's easy to forget that You have asked me to focus on only what is true, honorable, pure, and lovely. It's even easy to start contributing to the negative talk and negative mindset that seem to pervade our planet on many levels.

Forgive me for allowing negative thoughts to permeate my mind. I know that what I think affects how I feel, what I say, and also what I do. If I want to live as a kingdom hero, I need to focus on positive thoughts steeped in faith, love, kindness, purity, and Your Word.

Thanksgiving

Thank You, Father, for outlining how I need to think. This is a great reminder when so much of the chatter circulating in our contemporary culture is negative. Thank You for reminding me of the importance of keeping my mind clean and free from the toxicity of negativity.

Thank You for revealing the direct correlation between what a person thinks and what that person is. For me to truly live as a kingdom hero, I must think kingdom hero-like thoughts. I must remove thoughts based on fear, doubt, hate, jealousy, envy, pride, anxiety, and self-preservation. Thank You, Lord, for revealing this life-hack truth so clearly.

Supplication

Jesus, I desire to live as a kingdom hero, and I know one way to ensure I do is through corralling my thoughts more intentionally so that I'm thinking what is in alignment with Your overarching truth, purity, and kingdom values.

I ask You to help me develop a more positive mindset. Help me navigate toward people and information that will help my thoughts remain positive. Give me the self-control to turn off negative influences and toxic, negative chatter. Give me a glimpse into how powerful positive thoughts can truly be in transforming difficulties in my life into good outcomes. Show me what I need to do to feed my mind and my thoughts with truth, and give me discernment to weed out the lies of the enemy.

In Christ's name I pray, amen.

38

PRAYING FOR A WILLINGNESS TO TAKE RISKS

*God has not given us a spirit of timidity, but
of power and love and discipline.*

2 TIMOTHY 1:7

Adoration

Father, risk-taking is not necessarily in Your character because You know the end from the beginning. You know the outcome before starting. But risk-taking is entirely necessary for me to live as a kingdom hero. Because in order to follow You, I need to take risks based on faith in what You are saying or have said. And because You are altogether faithful and truthful, in all honesty it's not a risk to follow You.

But many times following You feels like a risk simply because I can't see how things will turn out or what the next steps may be. But I worship You for allowing me the opportunity to grow and develop this character quality of risk-taking. I honor You for giving me the chance to learn and develop my risk muscles.

Confession

Lord, I confess that talking about taking risks is a whole lot easier than actually taking them. But I don't want timidity to determine what steps I take. I want Your power to manifest itself in all I do and say.

Forgive me for pulling back when You ask me to push forward. Forgive me for wanting to analyze what I do rather than relying on You and Your leading in my life. Forgive me for my lack of courage, power, love, and discipline. You have not given me a spirit of timidity. I know any timidity I sense comes from Satan or from my own flesh.

Thanksgiving

God, thank You for calling me to take risks of faith. Thank You for opening my heart up to what that means by studying characters in Scripture who took risks of faith. Help me learn more from them so I will grow in my own confidence to step out in faith. Show me what I need to do in order to discover how to live a life of risk based on Your Word and guidance.

Thank You for awakening in me a desire to learn more about how to be a kingdom hero in my everyday life—even if it means taking risks.

Supplication

God, give me boldness. Fill my heart, soul, and mind with courage. Give me the ability to overcome my fear of risk-taking or my desire for a perfectly scripted outcome for everything I do. Life is messy, and the kingdom heroes in the Bible did not have perfect lives.

You have not created me or called me to live according to my plans; You have created me and called me to live as a faith-filled believer willing to take the risks You ask me to take. Show me what risks to take. Confirm Your guidance and direction in my spirit through the ways that You do. Help me sharpen my mind in such a way that I'll be able to know when You are speaking to me and when You are asking me to do something in particular. And I pray for Your favor on the risks of faith I do take so I can learn from those experiences and grow in the midst of them.

In Jesus' name I pray, amen.

39

PRAYING FOR RESILIENCE TO OVERCOME SETBACKS

*In all these things we overwhelmingly
conquer through Him who loved us.*

ROMANS 8:37

Adoration

Lord God, Jesus has set the ultimate example of overcoming setbacks. There is no greater setback than to be nailed to a cross, crucified, and left to die by those you love and came to save. Yet Jesus didn't remain on the cross. He didn't remain in the state of death and decay. Instead, He rose. And because He rose, and because Jesus lives in me, I also have the ability to overcome any setback I face according to Your will. His presence in me is enough to inspire and strengthen me to overwhelmingly conquer whatever I face.

I praise, worship, and adore You not only for the salvation that comes through Jesus Christ—a salvation for eternity—but also for the empowering love He gives me in my everyday life.

Confession

My God in heaven, resilience isn't always what defines me. Sometimes life gets so hard that I want to pause and just sit out the next round. I want to be more resilient and live with the tenacity of a king-dom hero, but I have to admit that in the midst of fluctuating emotions, often based on circumstances, I don't always live up to my own hopes and expectations.

Forgive me for wavering when I do. Forgive me for throwing in the towel—or considering throwing it in far more often than I should. Grant me Your mercy so that I will feel emboldened to stop looking at my past failures and focus on the future opportunities to rebound, overcome, and push through.

Thanksgiving

Lord, thank You for Your model of resilience. Thank You for the kingdom heroes in Scripture who show me what it looks like to over-come setbacks. My heart is filled with gratitude for the lessons I can learn from those who have gone before me, for those who show what it means to never give up and never give in as Satan tries to sideline believers through just plain weariness and despair.

Thank You for the strength I can find in Jesus Christ, knowing it's enough to propel me into a walk of faith that will please You in every way.

Supplication

Holy Father, I pray for greater resilience to overcome life's setbacks. I pray that I will see myself as an overcomer. I ask for the ability to change my mindset on how I view potential issues in life. Help me view them as opportunities to overcome rather than as roadblocks to stop me in my life's pursuit.

Infuse me with the courage and resilience I need to move through life fully vested and fully present. I don't want to hide in the face of opposition. Rather, I want to boldly walk through the fire of testing and the winds of change so I can demonstrate the resilience and tenacity of a kingdom hero to those around me. Show me what I need to do in order to grow in this area of my life.

In Christ's name I pray, amen.

40

PRAYING FOR PERSISTENCE

*Let us not lose heart in doing good, for in due
time we will reap if we do not grow weary.*

GALATIANS 6:9

Adoration

God, I'm glad You never lost heart when You created the earth and
the universe and all they contain. I'm glad You never lost heart as Christ
hung on the cross to save humanity from our sinfulness and the eternal
damnation that comes with it. You have always been persistent about
what You set out to do, and I praise You for Your ability to embody
this kingdom value.

I honor You for Your persistence. I worship You for Your reliability. I lift Your name in praise as I consider the works of Your hands and
Your presence in keeping it all together. Great is Your name and worthy of all praise.

Confession

Father, forgive me for being fickle rather than faithful when it comes
to persistence in my kingdom walk as a follower and disciple of Jesus
Christ. Show me what I need to do in order to serve You more faithfully
and persistently with my life. I want to honor You, but I confess I sometimes make decisions that reflect a lack of reliable faithfulness to You.

Forgive me for falling back when times get tough. Forgive me for when I give up. Sometimes I've given up even when a situation started to slowly improve, simply because I lost interest. Help me remain steadfast and immovable so I don't miss out on opportunities to serve You and help others as I should.

Thanksgiving

God, thank You for reminding me of the need for me to be persistent in my walk of faith. To live as a kingdom hero, I need to model what it means to be committed to You and Your Word. I can't go back and forth in my thinking, swayed by popular opinion and giving in to my own flesh and desires. I need to honor You with what I do and say, so I thank You for Your Word revealing to me how to do that.

Help me push through to the finish line in all that I do for Your kingdom. Help me not to lose interest, giving me the persistence in my spirit I need to bring You glory. Thank You for empowering me to live my life as a kingdom hero who persistently pursues advancing Your kingdom agenda and expressing kingdom values on earth.

Supplication

Lord, help me learn from my inaction and mistakes. Help me discover how persistence in the Christian faith is crucial to living as a kingdom hero. I want to learn these lessons so I can apply the wisdom of what I learn. I ask You to teach me.

But please do not use painful situations to teach me. In Your mercy, teach me with grace and open my eyes and my heart to a quick understanding. Make me a fast learner in the areas I need to grow, especially in this area of persistence, Lord. Show me how what I learn will impact my life for good and improve the lives of those around me.

In Jesus' name I pray, amen.

41

PRAYING FOR GOOD THINGS

Every good thing given and every perfect gift is from
above, coming down from the Father of lights, with
whom there is no variation or shifting shadow.

JAMES 1:17

Adoration

Father, every good thing given to me and every perfect gift sent my way—whether favor, blessing, or wisdom—is from You. All good things come from Your hand because You are the source of all that is good.

I worship You and praise You for who You are and how You desire to bless those who follow You with goodness, grace, mercy, and favor. I honor Your name and ask that You receive my authentic praise. Every moment that brings me joy and pure happiness is from You, and I honor You for the way You love Your creation and those who call on Your name. You are God, King, Savior, and Lord.

Confession

Holy God, forgive me for far too often confusing the source of every good thing and every perfect gift. Forgive me for looking to and magnifying mankind rather than You or for looking to or exalting humanity rather than You.

Forgive me for even exalting myself and falling under the deception that I ushered in the goodness I experience in this life. It's all due to Your righteous, kind hand of favor and blessing, and I don't want to seek to usurp Your glory through my own arrogance or misplaced adoration.

Thanksgiving

Father, thank You for every good thing You have given me. Thank You for loving me and showing me what I need to do in order to experience the abundant life Christ sacrificed Himself for me to have and know.

Thank You for every perfect gift You have allowed me to experience and treasure. Thank You for the sunshine that brings energy to the earth and encourages life to grow. Thank You for the rain that also helps to produce the growth of life and sustains it in so many ways. Thank You for the gift of relationships that help me foster a deeper intimacy with You. Thank You for the gifts of church, family, fun, and food.

Supplication

Lord, I ask that You bless me with every good and perfect gift You want for me. I ask for Your favor and the floodgates of heaven to be opened to me with so many blessings and gifts from You that I am overwhelmed with gratitude. I ask that Your provision in my life will be a testimony to others of Your loving care so that they will also boldly pray to You and ask You to favor them as well as they seek You as Lord over their lives.

I also ask that Your many blessings and gifts strengthen me to live as a kingdom hero, making a difference in everything I do and leaving a lasting impact for good on everyone with whom I come into contact.

In Christ's name I pray, amen.

42

PRAYING FOR ASSURANCE

Jesus Christ is the same yesterday and today and forever.

Hebrews 13:8

Adoration

God Almighty, Jesus Christ is the reflection of who You are, and in Hebrews 13:8 we're told that He is the same yesterday, today, and forever. His unchanging character qualities reflect Your own. You are the changeless God who is always reliable, always dependable, always trustworthy, and always faithful. You do not change. While Your methods may change, Your core character values and Your essence never do and never will.

I worship You for the assurance I find in everyday life knowing that the God I serve changes not. In a world constantly changing with new rules, new issues, and new developments, I honor You for never moving with the tides. You are consistent, and in Your consistency I find the boldness and faith I need to fully live as a kingdom hero.

Confession

Holy Lord, I confess that even though You don't change and Jesus Christ is the same yesterday, today, and forever, I can often change on a dime. Forgive me for allowing situations, circumstances, or even my emotions to dictate changes in my thoughts, moods, and actions. Forgive me for the way my faith can fluctuate based on external events. I confess that, as Your kingdom follower, I don't reflect Your changeless character or ways as much as I should. So I ask for Your covering of mercy and grace to cleanse me from this lack and so much more.

Thanksgiving

Father, thank You for the assurance that comes in knowing that You are a God who is the same yesterday, today, and tomorrow. I don't need to wake up each day and determine who You are choosing to be or what You are choosing to emphasize.

You don't resemble cancel culture, which changes as quickly as the seasons. You have made it clear in Your Word what Your kingdom values are and what the consequences of sin are as well. I don't have to guess about cause-and-effect outcomes based on my choices. You have told me what You esteem and what You condemn. Thank You for the assurance and peace this brings to me in knowing I can rest in my understanding of You.

Supplication

God, I ask that the assurance that comes from knowing You are in control, that You are sovereign, and that You don't change brings me greater calm. So much is going on in our world today that can provoke chaotic feelings inside.

But when I think of You, I find the assurance I'm looking for in order to truly rest. My spirit can rest when I remember the assurance of Your love. I don't have to guess if You love me; I'm assured that You love me. I don't need to guess if You are present; I know You are present. Your presence does not change. I'm assured of Your power, so I know I can also tap into Your power when I choose to pursue You according to Your overarching rule and governing in my life.

Give me the gift of peace in my spirit and in my emotions as I live according to the full awareness of the assurance of who You are as King of kings and Lord of lords over all.

In Jesus' name I pray, amen.

43

PRAYING FOR PHYSICAL STRENGTH

*The LORD will give strength to His people; the
LORD will bless His people with peace.*

PSALM 29:11

Adoration

Father, the strongest of the strong could not stand up against You.
They are no match for You. You are greater than the greatest who has
ever lived.

While humanity knows limits of physical strength, You do not.
Your strength holds all things together in love. You are a mighty God.
Mountains quake at the sound of Your voice. The strongest towers
built by mankind could not last even a moment if You chose to bring
them down. Nothing on this earth can remain apart from Your desire
to allow it simply due to Your strength.

The strength of Your might is a force to be reckoned with, and I
praise and worship You for Your powerful arm.

Confession

God, even though You are stronger than anything that exists in this
world, I somehow tend to forget this. Especially when the storms of

life crash in on me, I tend to look at the power of the storm rather than to Your strength. But if I were to look to Your strength, I would know where to find my own. My strength is found in Christ alone. Whether physical, spiritual, or mental strength, the source of it is You.

Forgive me for relying on myself or on those I look to for help rather than turning to You directly to give me the physical strength I need to face whatever challenges come my way. Forgive me for seeking to maneuver and build the purposes You have given me through my own strength rather than using the strength You supply to me.

Thanksgiving

Father, thank You for the gift of physical strength. I take so much for granted, and this is probably one of the most important. The physical strength You have given me has enabled me to do so much in my life I otherwise never could.

I'm able to pursue my passions and purpose in large part due to the physical strength and stamina You have provided me. I'm able to bring You glory in my actions due to the physical strength You have given me. Thank You, God, for my physical body and the blessings I have in using it, developing it, and nurturing it for further growth.

Supplication

God, I ask for greater physical strength. I ask for the ability to overcome weakness and lethargy. Give me wisdom and insight for how to nourish myself with food, rest, and exercise so I can develop the body You gave me for optimum, peak performance.

Show me what I can do to reach a greater level of physical strength, and give me a glimpse of why greater physical strength will help me live out my calling as a kingdom hero. I pray for opportunities and motivation to exercise. I pray against the spirit and emotions that lead to laziness. I ask for Your strength to be made manifest both in and through me so that I can truly live out the plan for my life You have placed me here to fulfill.

In Christ's name I pray, amen.

44

PRAYING FOR EXCELLENT HEALTH

Beloved, I pray that in all respects you may prosper
and be in good health, just as your soul prospers.

3 John 1:2

Adoration

Holy God, health is such an important part of life and the ability to be productive. I praise You and worship You for providing all that is needed for our bodies to stay healthy here on earth.

You have created food for us to eat, which supplies vitamins, minerals, and important nutrients for our biological systems. You have given us sunshine to invigorate us and make us healthy. Not only that, but You have made these things available to us in ways that are a delight to take in. The variety of Your creation amazes me, and I praise You for the attention to all of the details You have supplied. You are the creator of all I need in order to live a healthy life.

Confession

Father, You have made my body to function so well. You have provided me with an immune system to fight off ailments and germs. You have crafted me with such intricacies that I can't even fathom what all has to take place for eating, breathing, digesting, and more.

Yet I confess that I don't always give You the thanks and the glory

You deserve for Your gift of life to me. Forgive me for the times I neglect my body through unhealthy consumption or laziness. My body is a gift from You that enables me to fully live out my purpose, but I have taken it for granted far too often and failed to intentionally focus on how to live at my healthiest state of being. Forgive me for this, and cover me with Your cleansing and pure love and grace.

Thanksgiving

God, thank You for my physical health. Thank You for every day I have lived on this earth without pain or serious ailments. Thank You for creating my body in such a way that it literally fights off germs and sicknesses without my even knowing it is. You are so comprehensive in how You have created and designed the human body.

Thank You for the moments and seasons of excellent health, and thank You for prompting me to pray for more of them. When I'm in great health, I have access to the physical, mental, and emotional energy I need to carry out Your plan for my life. I love You and praise You for giving me the gift of good health each time You have done so.

Supplication

God, I ask for excellent health. I ask for the grace sent from above that will enable my body to be healthy, strong, vibrant, full of energy, and able to fend off illness. I pray for the ability, interest, and wisdom to eat food that will strengthen my body and keep me in a state of optimum health.

Show me what I need to do by way of exercise to also help my body be as healthy as it possibly can. Help my cells, my blood, and my organs to function at the levels of health You have designed them to do, and keep me from doing anything to my body that will harm me or harm my health in any way.

In Jesus' name I pray, amen.

45

PRAYING FOR MENTAL CLARITY

*You hypocrite, first take the log out of your own eye, and then
you will see clearly to take the speck out of your brother's eye.*

Matthew 7:5

Adoration

Holy God, judgment clouds a mind. It prevents people from thinking clearly because judgment is hypocritical when focused on someone else's sin apart from their own. A true kingdom hero doesn't live in a spirit of mental confusion or mess, always thinking about what other people have done or said wrong.

But in Your Word You have clearly told us how to gain mental clarity—through removing the log from our own eye before looking to others'. I praise You for always showing us how to wisely live a productive life as a kingdom hero in Your Word. I honor You for teaching us through so much truth made available in Scripture, which guides and directs us on how to live and have a healthy, spiritual mindset.

Confession

God, I confess that it's easier to allow my mind to be clouded over with thoughts of what others are doing wrong than to focus on how I need to improve my own life and actions. It's easier to blame others than to take responsibility for my own failings.

Forgive me for choosing the lazy path of mental exercise, which judges or condemns the culture or people around me rather than examines the chaos within me brought about by my own sin. Forgive me for failing to take the log out of my own eye yet rushing to dig specks out of the eyes of those around me or people in our culture, such as politicians and celebrities.

Thanksgiving

Father, thank You for the gift of mental clarity and for the direction and guidance on how to achieve it on a regular basis. Thank You for wisdom that shows me what I need to do in order to live as a kingdom hero. Thank You for Your grace and forgiveness that serve as models for the grace and forgiveness I ought to extend to others.

I was created for good works, and if those good works involve helping others to remove the specks in their eyes, please remind me to first remove the log from my own eye. Remind me to always speak and act with a spirit of humility, recognizing that no one is better than anyone else, that we are all made righteous through the sacrifice of Jesus Christ on the cross.

Supplication

God, I ask for greater mental clarity. I ask for the self-control I need to turn off the TV, or stop scrolling on social media, or give myself the space I need to allow my thoughts to be authentic, spiritual, and pure.

I ask for a greater recognition of my own personal sins so I don't waste my life in a state of false pride. Pride clouds the mind and twists thoughts so they are no longer pure. Your Word says that the pure in heart will see You. I believe this also means the pure in mind. I ask that I will be both pure in heart and pure in mind so that I can truly see You and Your hand of involvement in my daily life.

In Christ's name I pray, amen.

46

PRAYING FOR SPIRITUAL CLARITY

Open my eyes, that I may behold wonderful things from Your law.

PSALM 119:18

Adoration

Father, You see things clearly. And because You do, You always know how to make the right decisions for the greater good of all involved. I know that because I trust in You, I can go to You to seek greater spiritual clarity in my life. I praise You, for You are a great and holy God who knows the end from the beginning and every step that should be taken in order to get there.

You know where to lead me, and I want to tap into Your great wisdom more. I worship You for making Yourself and Your wisdom available for the asking. I honor You for the power of Your mind, for the purity of Your heart, and for the vision of Your Spirit.

Confession

Father, issues in life don't always look crystal clear to me. I try to discern or make decisions, but I lack the spiritual clarity You have.

Forgive me for jumping ahead of Your leading and trying to operate by my own standards and my own wisdom. Forgive me for failing to stop and take the time to clear my mind of the clutter of this world. Reveal to me the power of Your forgiveness and grace by helping me become more attuned to Your guidance.

Thanksgiving

Holy God, thank You for the access to spiritual clarity You provide me. Thank You for showing me how I can access it through prayer and meditation on Your Word. I give You thanks for causing my heart to soften spiritually and my soul to mature and develop at such a level that I can hear Your Spirit's leading.

Thank You for the opportunity to pray and ask You to show me the best steps to take. Thank You for touching my heart in such a way that prompted me to pick up this book of guided prayers. Thank You for motivating me to read and use it, thus developing my spiritual walk more and more with every prayer. Thank You for everyone who had a hand in putting this book together so that others can benefit from these prayers.

Supplication

God, I ask for greater spiritual clarity so I can discern truth from lies. I also ask for the ability to identify Your voice and weed out the chatter from the enemy or from TV or social media—and even from my own thoughts or from the voices of those with whom I'm in a relationship.

Show me how to receive Your guidance in a way that gives me confidence to pursue it and follow You in faith like a kingdom hero. I've tried to make my own decisions and failed for far too long. I want to be sensitive to the Spirit's leading and direction so I can maximize the life You have given me. I ask You to shower me with the blessing of spiritual clarity and sensitivity to You like I've never known before.

In Jesus' name I pray, amen.

47

PRAYING FOR MORE LOVE

*Beloved, let us love one another, for love is from God; and
everyone who loves is born of God and knows God. The one
who does not love does not know God, for God is love.*

1 JOHN 4:7-8

Adoration

Holy God, we are called to love one another because You are love.
Hatred does not originate with You; it originates with Satan. Bitterness
does not reflect You; it reflects Satan. Resentment does not come from
Your heart; it comes from the devil himself. Yet our culture seems to
promote division, hatred, bitterness, and resentment in so many ways,
and Satan uses these tools to keep us from the high purpose of love
because love represents You.

Those who love know You. Those who do not love do not know
You. I worship You and honor You for Your heart of love and Your call
to love those who seek to live as Your kingdom followers.

Confession

God, I know a true kingdom hero loves. A true kingdom hero
doesn't spend time thinking, saying, or posting negative things about
others because that is not reflective of love.

So many people have turned away from You and the Christian

faith because too many claim to know You yet do not know You, as evidenced in their lack of love. Forgive me for every time I've fallen into that category. Forgive me for every time I've chosen hate over love, judgment over acceptance, resentment over forgiveness. Forgive me for harboring thoughts of blame rather than thoughts of trust in Your sovereign hand. Forgive me even for those times when I've failed to love myself as the magnificent human being made in Your image I am.

Thanksgiving

Thank You, God, for the call to love. Thank You for modeling love and for being a God who desires His followers to love. Without love, this world would be a mess. Where there is an absence of love, it already is a mess. Thank You for the healing power of love.

Thank You for defining for us what love practically and actually looks like in 1 Corinthians 13, where You tell us that love is patient, kind, not arrogant, and thinks of others first. You have made it clear to us how to love and what love entails. Thank You for the clarity of Your holy Word, which guides and prods me toward the highest purpose of mankind—to love others as You have loved.

Supplication

Lord, please fill me with Your love to such a degree that it overflows to those around me. Let me be the reflection of Your love in a world that needs love so badly. Show me ahead of time what I can do to demonstrate Your love to those in need. Give me greater love in my tone of voice, in my patience with others, and even toward myself.

Love is Your essence, and that love holds all things together in the person of Jesus Christ. Your love is the strongest weapon in the hands of a kingdom hero. With love, we can defeat the enemy's schemes and turn back his advances. Raise up an army of heroes who choose love, kindness, joy, and peace. Let love cast out hate. Let light remove the darkness on this earth.

In Christ's name I pray, amen.

48

PRAYING FOR SPIRITUAL MATURITY

Though by this time you ought to be teachers, you have need again for someone to teach you the elementary principles of the oracles of God, and you have come to need milk and not solid food. For everyone who partakes only of milk is not accustomed to the word of righteousness, for he is an infant. But solid food is for the mature, who because of practice have their senses trained to discern good and evil.

HEBREWS 5:12-14

Adoration

Holy God, You desire that each of us grows and develops spiritually. That's because as we do, we're able to reflect You more and live as the kingdom heroes You created us to be. Growing spiritually is not necessarily easy. As we see in studying the lives of the kingdom heroes in Scripture, spiritual growth often comes through hard lessons that need to be learned. Wilderness seasons are difficult to go through, but those are the times when we can learn so much.

You are a God who doesn't spoil Your followers so that we never have opportunities to learn and develop spiritual maturity. I praise You for Your patience in allowing us to learn and grow, even when times feel tough for us, because You know that in the long run that growth will produce a greater return overall.

Confession

God, I confess that I don't care for the times of development in my life. They aren't my favorite seasons. Wilderness wanderings or difficult challenges may produce a greater spiritual hunger and maturity, but I admit that I complain, whine, or feel despondent in those times more than I should.

Forgive me for failing to recognize Your faithfulness in these times of spiritual growth. Also please forgive me for those times when I don't even desire to grow spiritually but am content with being stagnant where I am. The kingdom walk requires maturity. No kingdom heroes ever accomplished all they were built for by remaining spiritually lazy. Forgive me for any spiritual laziness I demonstrate and live out.

Thanksgiving

Lord God, thank You for honoring me with the opportunity and calling to grow and develop spiritually. Thank You for surrounding me with a church or relationships or podcasts or books or other resources to help me grow and learn more about what it means to live as a kingdom hero.

I never run out of opportunities to grow, and so I want to give You thanks for Your consistent involvement in my heart, in my mind, and in my spirit, which all prompts me to look to You as the catalyst for my personal growth. Thank You for opening up my heart to greater possibilities as Your follower. I know You have tremendous plans for my life, and I want to mature to the point where I can truly fulfill them.

Supplication

God, help me pursue spiritual growth as passionately as I should in order to achieve my full spiritual potential. Teach me what it means to be a consistent, dedicated, and dependable kingdom hero. Bring people into my life who will sharpen me spiritually. I also ask You to surround me with people into whom I can pour and help to grow and mature spiritually.

Guide me to the books and other resources that will help me in my spiritual walk and show me what I can do to keep myself on a trajectory of spiritual growth toward maturity.

In Jesus' name I pray, amen.

PRAYING FOR
MORE TIME IN GOD'S WORD

*Putting aside all malice and all deceit and hypocrisy and
envy and all slander, like newborn babies, long for the pure
milk of the word, so that by it you may grow in respect to
salvation, if you have tasted the kindness of the Lord.*

1 Peter 2:1-3

Adoration

God, in Your Word You have given me all I need for my life. Every
ounce of wisdom, guidance, and hope is found in its pages. And You
have blessed me with access to Your Word when so many in the world
don't have that. I never want to take this blessing for granted.

I lift Your name in praise, and I worship You for supplying me
with truth. You oversaw the writing and compilation of Your Word
through men moved by Your Holy Spirit. Your working through and
with humanity in this way reveals the power of Your perfection. Every
word in the Scriptures is truth and contains life. Your Word is living
and breathing and able to be used as part of the armor we need to overcome the enemy and his lies.

Confession

Father, Jesus, and Spirit, You are found in the Word, and I can get to know You in the Word. Forgive me for neglecting Scriptures as much as I do. Forgive me for failing to turn to Your Word for the hope I need when I'm feeling down.

I ask for Your forgiveness for failing to make the most use of Your Word as I possibly can. Forgive my laziness when it comes to meditating on Your Word. Forgive my lack of willingness to apply the truth of Scripture to every area of my life. Forgive me for spending so much time in frivolity and entertainment yet so little time in the reading of Your Word.

Thanksgiving

Thank You, Lord, for Your Word, which gives healing to my heart and hope to my spirit. Thank You for the immediate access I have to Your Word whenever I want to read it. Thank You for raising up all of the preachers and teachers who spend time studying Your Word in order to deliver a deeper understanding of it to those who listen.

Thank You for the desire in my heart to learn and apply Your Word in my life. I ask You to receive the gratitude of my heart for all that Your Word gives me. It helps me know how to live as a kingdom hero because of the countless examples You have granted us throughout its pages.

Supplication

God, help me better prioritize spending time in Your Word. Help me better strategize the use of my time so that I have more time to dedicate to learning, studying, meditating, and memorizing it. I want to know You more, and one of the ways I can do that is through my heart and mind's immersion into Your Word.

Please help me find and use tools that will enable me to experience and understand Your Word more. Guide me in the path of greater biblical study so I feel confident as I go through the various books of Your Scripture and seek to know and identify Your heart, Your values, and Your purposes throughout. I ask for wisdom from Your Word.

In Christ's name I pray, amen.

PRAYING FOR GREATER OPPORTUNITIES FOR EVANGELISM

*[Jesus] said to them, "Go into all the world
and preach the gospel to all creation."*

MARK 16:15

Adoration

Father, You have told us as Your kingdom followers to go into all the world and preach the gospel to all creation. You have made it clear what the primary purpose of a kingdom disciple truly is. We're to take the gospel of Jesus Christ, the saving power of His salvation, to a world in need. And in sharing the gospel, we get to experience Your power and the presence of Your Spirit like never before.

As Peter shared the gospel to 3,000, he became bold like never before. You empower what You call us to do, and You have asked us to evangelize. I praise You for the offer of salvation You make available to anyone who calls on the name of the Lord Jesus Christ for the forgiveness of sin in order to be saved.

Confession

God, forgive me for the times I haven't evangelized when You gave me the opportunity. Forgive me for feeling hesitant to speak about the gospel when the open door is in front of me.

Show me how I can grow in my confidence to share the gospel with others. Cleanse me of whatever might be holding me back—like pride, doubt, or a desire for acceptance from others. Forgive the unease and even shame that creeps up when it shouldn't. Paul said he was not ashamed of the gospel, and yet too often my mouth has remained closed when I've been given the chance to share the saving news of Jesus Christ.

Thanksgiving

Lord God, thank You for the high calling to evangelize. Thank You that Jesus Christ came to earth to bear the punishment for my sins and for the sins of all humanity. Thank You that a gospel even exists to share. You are a gracious, loving God who supplies everything we need, including our entrance into eternity through faith alone in Christ alone for the forgiveness of sins.

Thank You for choosing me to bear witness of Your love and saving power so I can be an ambassador for Jesus wherever I go. Thank You for saving me from my sins and cleansing me from all unrighteousness so the boldness from which I speak and share the gospel comes from a right alignment with the Holy Spirit within me. You have empowered me to do what You have asked me to do when I align myself underneath your overarching kingdom rule.

Supplication

Father, I ask You to provide me with opportunities to share the gospel with others. Give me boldness in my speech. Supply a passion within me to see other people come to know You as their Lord and Savior. Help me develop relationships with nonbelievers so I can have the opportunity to witness to them.

Show me creative ways to use the life and talents You've given me in order to proclaim Your gospel to anyone who needs to hear it. Please also guide and direct me on how I can invest in and support ministries that share the gospel or translate it for those who have not yet heard of the saving power of Jesus Christ in their own language.

In Jesus' name I pray, amen.

51

PRAYING FOR INSIGHT INTO BIBLICAL JUSTICE

He has told you, O man, what is good; and what
does the LORD require of you but to do justice, to love
kindness, and to walk humbly with your God?

MICAH 6:8

Adoration

Heavenly Father, You desire us to do what is good, and You have made what is good clear in Your Word. You have told us what You require of us as Your followers—to do justice, love kindness, and walk with humility. Your character is pure, and Your heart is full of love for all You have made.

When we treat one another with injustice, it hurts You. It damages the reflection of Your image in mankind. Injustice to one is injustice to all because we're made to mirror and honor You through our lives and choices. I honor and worship You for the pureness of who You are and the depth of love You have for every person on this planet.

Confession

Lord, I confess that unless they're impacting me personally, I often ignore issues of injustice in our culture at large. I can become so self-absorbed with my own life and my own desires that I forget that many millions of people face injustices in their daily lives.

Forgive me for failing to take notice and failing to speak up and defend the rights of those who experience injustice. Forgive me for failing to pray for biblical justice everywhere and for the dignity of humanity to be upheld through how we treat one another. Forgive me for when I lack kindness toward others as well.

Thanksgiving

Thank You, God, that You have called me to live a higher standard than selfishness or undue introspection. You have called me to be a beacon of light in a dark world. In fact, You haven't just called me to pursue biblical justice for those who need it; You require me to live it. This is considered good in Your sight.

Thank You for Your heart, which teaches my heart how I should take seriously the injustices plaguing our communities, our nation, and the world. Thank You for giving me a voice to speak up and actions I can take to educate myself and seek to make a positive impact for Your name and Your kingdom agenda of biblical justice on earth.

Supplication

Father, help me make better use of my time, my thoughts, and also my prayers on behalf of those who suffer from injustices. And where I suffer from injustices in my daily life, help me stand up for myself but to do so in a spirit of love and kindness.

Show me ways to truly make a lasting impact for good in our land and on all those around me. Open my eyes and my heart to the injustices that swarm society and seek to manipulate and oppress people. I ask for wisdom on how to inspire others to rise up and defend biblical justice through their words and actions as well. Make me a vessel for Your grace, Your love, Your mercy, and biblical justice to flow through.

In Christ's name I pray, amen.

52

PRAYING FOR INTIMACY WITH GOD

Abide in Me, and I in you. As the branch cannot bear fruit of itself unless it abides in the vine, so neither can you unless you abide in Me. I am the vine, you are the branches; he who abides in Me and I in him, he bears much fruit, for apart from Me you can do nothing.

JOHN 15:4-5

Adoration

I come to You, Lord, knowing that You desire an intimate relationship with me. You have made it clear that only in such a relationship will I discover my purpose, power, and peace. You have blessed me with this opportunity to live as a kingdom hero simply by drawing near to You and abiding in You.

You have made it so clear that there really is no confusion or secret to how to access all that I need to fully realize my destiny and purpose on earth. I praise You and worship You for the glory of who You are and Your willingness to share Your heart with me intimately. You are a mighty God who dwells high in the heavens but is also willing to dwell low with humanity as close as we'll allow You to be.

Confession

Lord, I have read Your Word, and I know the secret to the abundant life and the fulfilling of my life's purpose. I know what it takes to move mountains in faith or produce fruit that lasts for the kingdom. Yet even though I know these truths in my mind, I don't always apply them in my actions.

Forgive me for neglecting my relationship with You and for not drawing near to You as I should. Forgive me for getting so busy that I forget to even speak to You from time to time. Forgive me for failing to slow down and take in the majesty of Your creation and the awesomeness of who You are, as well as failing to take in the fact that You even allow me to draw close to You. Cleanse me from shortsightedness and purify me from selfishness.

Thanksgiving

God, thank You for the invitation to abide in Christ so that Christ can abide in me. Thank You for giving me Your Word as a channel through which I can access Your heart, Your thoughts, and Your presence. Thank You for the gift of the Holy Spirit, who makes it possible for me to draw near to You and experience You in my life.

I want to take this calling and urging of Yours more seriously, because I know if I do, I'll benefit and those around me will benefit. You have said so in Your Word. Thank You for making it so clear and giving me the heart to hear and the spirit to tune in to what is truly important in life.

Supplication

Heavenly Father, I want to abide in You more fully. I want to feel Your presence and Your peace as I bask in Your love. Show me what it means to truly abide in You. Show me when I'm distracted. Point out how I can let go of certain things that aren't benefiting me at all.

I ask for Your wisdom to manifest itself in my life through a deeper, more intimate relationship with You. Draw me to You with Your love and Your favor so I may experience the joy of intimate fellowship with the one Creator God.

In Jesus' name I pray, amen.

53

PRAYING FOR BOLDNESS IN MY SPEECH

They spent a long time there speaking boldly with reliance upon the Lord, who was testifying to the word of His grace, granting that signs and wonders be done by their hands.

Acts 14:3

Adoration

God, You used boldness in Your speech when You spoke the worlds into existence. You were not ashamed. You didn't hold back. You didn't question or wonder what other people would think, say, or do. You didn't fear. You didn't doubt. You are an example of boldness in speech.

When Jesus hung on the cross, He boldly asked You to forgive those who didn't know what they were doing. He used boldness as He walked on earth, teaching people about the kingdom of God. Jesus boldly thanked You for blessing the loaves and fish before breaking it and feeding thousands with it.

I praise You and worship You for the boldness in which You function and make Your will known throughout the world.

Confession

God, I wish I always spoke with the boldness You have and Jesus used when He was on earth. I confess I don't always do so. Even when

I pray in public before a meal, sometimes I pray extra quietly or I wonder what the people around me might be thinking.

Forgive me for my lack of boldness in standing up for righteousness and kingdom values in our land. Forgive me for my lack of boldness in sharing the gospel with those in need. Forgive me for failing to speak with boldness when I need to in order to advance Your kingdom agenda on earth through the time, talents, and treasures You have given me.

Thanksgiving

Thank You, God, for reminding me through Acts 14:3 that my ability to speak with boldness comes from my reliance on You. If I try to speak boldly out of my own strength, I will fail. Only when I draw close to You and rely on You will I find the courage and boldness to speak the truth people need to hear. Help me reflect on this truth and meditate on it more fully so I truly understand and apply it in my life.

Thank You for the boldness You are willing to give me and the impact I can make as a kingdom hero when I choose to honor You through confident speech.

Supplication

Father, give me greater boldness in my speech. Help me to never waver in speaking truth in love when it's needed. I want to proclaim Your gospel whenever I can. I want to help others discover more about You through what I say. Show me how I can use my voice for Your glory and others' good as well as to advance Your kingdom principles on earth.

I ask for clarity in my thoughts so that when I do speak boldly, what I say will be clear to those who hear me. I ask for wisdom and spiritual maturity so that my speech is seasoned with grace and makes an impact on people's lives. Show me what I need to do in order to rely more on You as I look to live as a kingdom hero, willing and able to boldly speak the truths of Your Word and the power of Your gospel to everyone who needs to hear it.

In Christ's name I pray, amen.

54

PRAYING FOR SELF-CONTROL

*For this very reason also, applying all diligence, in your faith
supply moral excellence, and in your moral excellence, knowledge,
and in your knowledge, self-control, and in your self-control,
perseverance, and in your perseverance, godliness, and in your
godliness, brotherly kindness, and in your brotherly kindness, love.*

2 PETER 1:5-7

Adoration

Father God, I've learned that self-control is crucial to living as a
kingdom hero. It serves as a foundational character quality. Without it,
so much has the potential to go wrong or get off track. Thank You for
revealing this to me in Your Word. You have outlined the various kingdom qualities I need to live out my purpose in passages such as 2 Peter
1:5-7, which includes self-control.

I worship You and honor You for Your desire to communicate so
clearly with me through Your Word so that I don't lack an understanding of what You desire of me and how to fulfill it in my life. I lift
up Your name in praise because You are truly worthy of all praise and
adoration.

Confession

Lord, I confess that when I lack self-control, my life gets out of hand. I make mistakes or I harm relationships. I even harm my own potential when I lack the self-control necessary to live out the full manifestation of kingdom values.

Forgive me for my impulsiveness. Forgive me for my indulgences. Forgive me for failing to understand how important self-control truly is to maximizing my own potential. Selfishness may seem good or feel nice for a season, but it doesn't produce the lasting fruit that reflects a life of kingdom impact. Cleanse my heart and purify my thoughts so that my actions more reflect Your character.

Thanksgiving

Thank You, holy God, for the ability to live with self-control as provided to me through the power of the Holy Spirit. Thank You that I have all I need to make wise choices with my thoughts, with my words, and with my actions. I don't have to give in to emotional impulses or desires.

You have supplied me with both the instruction and ability to live a life pleasing to You as outlined in Your Word. Thank You for clearly articulating how I can honor You and impact others for good. The foundation of the kingdom hero's life is faith built on the pillars of self-control. Thank You for calling me to a life that reflects Your image through modeling the principles and qualities of kingdom values.

Supplication

Lord, help me have better self-control, whether related to my spending choices, to my entertainment options, to what I say, or to what I do. Show me the benefits of living with self-control so I can quickly learn and apply these lessons. Surround me with people who model spiritually healthy self-control so I can witness how Your favor is manifested in their lives and be encouraged by it.

Our culture doesn't promote self-control. In fact, it promotes the opposite. Give me strength to resist cultural temptations, knowing that my wise choices will set me up for success but following worldly wisdom is a recipe for disaster.

In Jesus' name I pray, amen.

55

PRAYING FOR ASSURANCE OF DIRECTION

*Lead me in Your truth and teach me, for You are the
God of my salvation; for You I wait all the day.*

Psalm 25:5

Adoration

Holy God, Your favor is life to me. Your confirmation in my daily walk provides peace and clarity. I don't always make the right decisions or the wisest choices. I'm human, and I lack the knowledge of all things that You have. You see the end from the beginning, so when I'm making a foolish decision, You know about it as it's happening. That's why I honor You for who You are and the knowledge You have.

I worship You for Your infinite wisdom, and I ask that it be poured into my life. Only because of Your favor will I live as a kingdom hero and maximize my life purpose on this earth. I lift up Your name in praise, knowing that You are the source of all wisdom, of all understanding, and the assurance of direction.

Confession

God, I confess that I've made a lot of decisions in my life and vocation, including with my finances, based on my own thoughts and understanding. If I had listened to Your leading, I would be so much further along. But I confess this to You, and I ask Your forgiveness. I don't want this pattern to continue. I want to walk in the favor of Your confirmation of my path. I want to take steps forward in my finances, in my vocation, and in all I do because I've learned to both listen to You and to rely on You.

Cleanse me from the pride that causes me to look to my own thinking before seeking Yours. These have been hard lessons to learn, Lord, but I choose now to follow You and Your leading first, and I want You to see that I do.

Thanksgiving

Thank You, God, for being willing to lead me in the direction I need to go. Thank You for speaking to me and guiding me along the way. Thank You for Your favor, which is life to my bones and prosperity to my soul. Make my way full of Your abundances and provision. Mark my steps so they are productive strides that lead to great gain.

Thank You for honoring me with Your ability to lead me. Thank You for allowing me to reach my full potential as a kingdom hero when I look to You as my guide, aligning myself under Your rule as Lord.

Supplication

Father, bless me with Your favor. Pour it down on my soul and my mind so my steps are ordered according to Your wisdom and plan. Confirm for me the work of my hands so all I do and invest in produces a great return. Show me how to use my time; my skills, talents, and gifts; and my treasures from You for gain. Keep me from loss.

Also help me enjoy the fruit of my work and to rest in the assurance that Your favor directed me to this place of success. Help me always speak of You when people ask how I have been so blessed and how I was able to find a life path that brings me so much joy and personal satisfaction. Help me always give You the glory for Your direction to this place.

In Christ's name I pray, amen.

56

PRAYING FOR PERSONAL PEACE

*The steadfast of mind You will keep in perfect
peace, because he trusts in You.*

Isaiah 26:3

Adoration

Holy God, You are perfect, and You are holy. You are righteous
and mighty. Your understanding is above all else. And because of the
greatness of Your love, I have the opportunity to find personal peace.
Because of the consistency of Your power, I have the gift of life itself.

I worship You and praise You, for You are a mighty God, worthy of
my gratitude. You sit above the earth and look down on the choices we
make, knowing which ones will produce better outcomes and which
ones will not. Yet You have chosen to give us free will, and with that
free will comes the consequences of our decisions. But Your patience
gives me the power to develop personal peace when my choices more
reflect Your character and heart.

Confession

God, personal peace comes through trusting in You. I know I can
trust in You because of Your history with me, the truth of Your Word,

and the power of Your presence. Yet sometimes I don't trust in You, and as a result, I face difficulties. I face internal chaos and unrest.

Forgive me for lacking a level of trust that produces personal peace. Forgive me for clinging to my own thoughts of worry and concern rather than seeking to replace them with the assurance of Your Word and the calming essence of Your presence.

Thanksgiving

Thank You, God, for Your desire that I live my life as a kingdom hero filled with the perfect peace that comes from trusting in You. Thank You for teaching me and training me according to Your wisdom and truth. Thank You for the gift of Your holy Word available to me each day. I can turn to Your Word whenever I need to be reminded of the strength of who You are.

Thank You, God, for the power of Your Word.

Supplication

Father, I ask for a greater willingness on my part to trust in You. I ask that the chains that bind me to my own desire for personal control and power be broken and stripped away. Show me what it means to discover the peace of Your presence, and guide me into a greater awareness of how to trust You.

Teach me Your Word on a larger scale so I can both better understand it and apply it to every situation I face. I want to honor You with a peaceful spirit, and I want to reflect You to others so I can be an example of kingdom living in a dark and chaotic world. Help me be the light of Your love and peace to those in my family, in my community, in my church, and in the world through all I do and say. But I know it all starts with my first finding personal peace internally by choosing to trust in You.

In Jesus' name I pray, amen.

57

PRAYING FOR BLESSING

Now it shall be, if you diligently obey the LORD your God, being careful to do all His commandments which I command you today, the LORD your God will set you high above all the nations of the earth. All these blessings will come upon you and overtake you if you obey the LORD your God: Blessed shall you be in the city, and blessed shall you be in the country. Blessed shall be the offspring of your body and the produce of your ground and the offspring of your beasts, the increase of your herd and the young of your flock. Blessed shall be your basket and your kneading bowl. Blessed shall you be when you come in, and blessed shall you be when you go out.

DEUTERONOMY 28:1-6

Adoration

Holy God, all blessings and good things come from You. You are the source of everything good, right, and holy in my life. Thank You for blessing me as much as You have. Thank You for helping me realize Your blessings each day.

I worship You as I consider the works of Your hands and the ways You have blessed me with peace, provisions, time, talents, skills, spiritual gifts, desires, relationships, experiences, and so much more. I honor You as the source of all that is good. I honor You for showing me in Your Word how I can gain even greater access into Your blessings each day.

Confession

God, even though You have made it abundantly clear how I can gain greater access into Your blessings, I still so often choose my own way. I still get caught up in trying to produce my own good and my own favor.

Forgive me for looking to myself or to other people to bless me. Forgive me for seeking other people's approval more than I seek Yours. Forgive me for trusting in the hands of humanity more than I trust in the hand of the almighty God who is the source of all growth, all grace, and all blessing in my life.

Thanksgiving

Thank You, God, for Your love and great care. Thank You for Your ability to bless me and to forgive me when I make mistakes or when I sin. Thank You for showing me how to please You. Thank You for so clearly stating in Your Word what I need to do in order to access Your blessings in my life.

You have said You will set me high above into the gifts of Your blessing if I'm careful to do all of Your commandments. Thank You for giving me commandments to protect me and prosper me if I will follow them. Thank You for showing me the way I can move forward with Your personal care made manifest in my life through an untold number of blessings.

Supplication

Father, I ask for Your wisdom in how to serve You more faithfully. I ask for a greater understanding and awareness of Your commandments so I can seek to obey You more fully. I know that as I do them, I will position myself for greater blessings from You.

Thank You for loving me like You do and for showing me how to please You as I seek to live my life as a kingdom hero would.

In Christ's name I pray, amen.

58

PRAYING FOR KINGDOM IMPACT

You are the salt of the earth; but if the salt has become tasteless,
how can it be made salty again? It is no longer good for anything,
except to be thrown out and trampled under foot by men. You
are the light of the world. A city set on a hill cannot be hidden;
nor does anyone light a lamp and put it under a basket, but on
the lampstand, and it gives light to all who are in the house. Let
your light shine before men in such a way that they may see
your good works, and glorify your Father who is in heaven.

MATTHEW 5:13-16

Adoration

Holy God, You have placed me here on earth as Your kingdom follower because You have a purpose for me to live out. I recognize the wisdom of Your purpose, and I want to honor You with all that I am. I worship You and praise You for how much You love me and desire to see me maximize my potential on earth.

Show me how I can do that for Your glory and to make a kingdom impact. Show me how to bring You greater glory through my choices. Receive the praises of my heart as I lift Your name in gratitude for my life, my skills, my talents, my gifts, and the purpose You have given me to live out so I can make a kingdom impact on all those I know or meet.

Confession

God, I confess that I haven't used my gifts, my talents, my skills, or my time as effectively as I could have in order to advance Your kingdom agenda on earth as much as possible. I want to leave a kingdom impact everywhere I go, and I want to make a difference in the lives of those with whom I come into contact, but sometimes I forget to focus on what matters most. I let myself be sidetracked by life's dramas or difficulties. Or I get pulled away by more pleasurable ways to spend my time.

Forgive me for neglecting this high calling of making a kingdom impact with my life.

Thanksgiving

Thank You, God, for blessing me with abilities that can truly make a difference in the lives of those around me. Thank You for allowing me open doors that have shown me how I can affect others for good and for Your glory. Thank You for inspiring my heart to such a degree that I want to use my life to its fullest in order to leave a lasting legacy of kingdom impact.

Thank You, too, for the people You put in my life who have shepherded me and mentored me and taught me, whether through their books, through their podcasts, through their other resources, or through their relationships with me.

Supplication

Father, show me how I can be a better steward of all You have blessed me with so I can make a kingdom impact with the time You have given me. Show me how to encourage others to live for You and pursue a deeper relationship with You. Bless my words with grace so what I say leaves people wanting to know more about You and who You are. Open doors for me so I can fully influence others for Your kingdom and glory.

In Jesus' name I pray, amen.

59

PRAYING FOR DISCERNMENT

Do not be conformed to this world, but be transformed by the
renewing of your mind, so that you may prove what the will
of God is, that which is good and acceptable and perfect.

ROMANS 12:2

Adoration

Holy God, You don't have to seek discernment. You have perfect clarity in all things. You have perfect understanding of all things. You are truth, so You are able to detect lies at face value.

I praise You for the perfection of who You are. I praise You for giving me the opportunity to renew my mind through the power of the Holy Spirit. I worship You because You are willing to give me the opportunity to abide in You and in Your Word in order to gain greater clarity.

Confession

God, I confess that I don't ask for discernment or seek it as often as I should. Had I sought discernment as much as I passionately pursued other things, I would be a lot further ahead in living out my purpose. I've wasted too much time in mistakes that You would have given me discernment to avoid had I asked You for it.

I don't want to be conformed to this world. I want to be transformed by the renewing of my mind so I can prove what Your will is for my life. Forgive me for those times when I've functioned outside of Your will.

Thanksgiving

Thank You, God, for the gift of the Holy Spirit, who makes it possible for my mind to be renewed as I seek to understand Your Word. Thank You for the gift of Your Word, which transforms my mind, my thoughts, and my perspective when I study it, meditate on it, and apply it. Thank You for urging me toward the path that will give me the greatest positive outcomes from a kingdom vantage point and for showing me how to live my life more effectively for Your kingdom agenda.

Through Your Word, I can demonstrate Your good, acceptable, and perfect will in my life.

Supplication

Father, help me grow in this area of discernment. Help me recognize the importance of discernment in my everyday life so I will long for it like I long for what is not as helpful.

Show me the power of discerning right from wrong. Show me which path to take. Give me opportunities to disciple others on this crucial kingdom principle and character quality. As I do, I know I will begin to move forward in my life to leave a legacy of kingdom influence. Show me what I need to do every step of the way, and allow me the patience to remain and abide in Your Word to such a degree that it molds and develops me into the person You have created me to be.

In Christ's name I pray, amen.

60

PRAYING FOR THE POWER
FROM GOD'S WORD

*The word of God is living and active and sharper than
any two-edged sword, and piercing as far as the division
of soul and spirit, of both joints and marrow, and able
to judge the thoughts and intentions of the heart.*

HEBREWS 4:12

Adoration

Holy God, as I come to the last guided prayer on the qualities and
character traits that make up a kingdom hero's life, I want to focus on
the power of Your Word. The Bible is the tool I need in order to overcome the enemy's schemes to keep me from living out my purpose.

I praise You for the way You have crafted Your Word and preserved
it over the years so people have access to it. You have also provided ways
for us to understand it. I praise You for raising up teachers and preachers who study Your Word and then help others learn from what they
have learned. I lift up Your name in humble praise as I consider the
enemy's many attempts to remove Your Word and the influence it has
on people's lives but also how You have prevented his success because
of Your great strength and sovereign power over all.

Confession

God, I don't read, meditate on, or memorize Your Word like I should. I don't spend as much time in Your Word as I ought. Your Word is the light to my path. It's what can guide me to a greater life of kingdom victory, and yet I too often don't take studying it seriously.

Forgive me for failing to cling to this resource You have given me with everything I am and with all the passion I have to pursue it. The power of Your Word is there for me to use at any time if I will but lift the sword of the Spirit and wield it as a kingdom hero can. Forgive me for neglecting so great a gift as the power of Your Word.

Thanksgiving

Thank You, God, for giving me all I need to overcome any obstacle that raises itself against me through the power of the Word of God. Thank You for calming my emotions when anxiety seeks to devour me—and for doing so through the truth of Your holy Word. Thank You for increasing my appetite for Your Word and surrounding me with so many great books, podcasts, churches, and small groups that can take me deeper into the study, understanding, and application of Your Word.

Supplication

Father, I ask for the power of Your Word to be my greatest tool. Its power can drive back Satan and his minions just by my using it. Jesus used Your Word to overcome the devil when he sought to throw Him off track. I can live as a kingdom hero when I choose to know, apply, and make use of Your Word according to the power within it. The Scriptures allow me to live out my fullest potential.

I want Your Word to always be fresh in my mind, close to my heart, and near to my emotions. Your Word is my guide. Your Word is my hope. Your Word is the power I need to live as the kingdom hero You have called me to be.

In Jesus' name I pray, amen.

THE URBAN ALTERNATIVE

The Urban Alternative (TUA) equips, empowers, and unites Christians to impact individuals, families, churches, and communities through a thoroughly kingdom-agenda worldview. In teaching truth, we seek to transform lives.

The core cause of the problems we face in our personal lives, homes, churches, and societies is a spiritual one. Therefore, the only way to address that core cause is spiritually. We've tried a political, social, economic, and even a religious agenda, and now it's time for a kingdom agenda.

The kingdom agenda can be defined as the visible manifestation of the comprehensive rule of God over every area of life.

The unifying central theme throughout the Bible is the glory of God and the advancement of His kingdom. The conjoining thread from Genesis to Revelation—from beginning to end—is focused on one thing: God's glory through advancing God's kingdom.

When we do not recognize that theme, the Bible becomes for us a series of disconnected stories that are great for inspiration but seem to be unrelated in purpose and direction. Understanding the role of the kingdom in Scripture increases our understanding of the relevancy of this several-thousand-year-old text to our day-to-day living. That's because God's kingdom was not only then; it is now.

The absence of the kingdom's influence in our personal lives, family lives, churches, and communities has led to a deterioration in our world of immense proportions:

- People live segmented, compartmentalized lives because they lack God's kingdom worldview.

- Families disintegrate because they exist for their own satisfaction rather than for the kingdom.

- Churches are limited in the scope of their impact because they fail to comprehend that the goal of the church is not its existence but its influencing the world for the kingdom.

- Communities have nowhere to turn to find real solutions for real people who have real problems because the church has become divided, ingrown, and unable to transform the cultural and political landscape in any relevant way.

By optimizing the solutions of heaven, the kingdom agenda offers us a way to see and live life with a solid hope. When God is no longer the final and authoritative standard under which all else falls, order and hope have left with Him. But the reverse is true as well: If God is still in the picture, and as long as His agenda is still on the table, we have hope. Even if relationships collapse, God will sustain us. Even if finances dwindle, God will keep us. Even if dreams die, God will revive us. As long as God and His rule are still the overarching standard in our lives, families, churches, and communities, hope remains.

Our world needs the King's agenda. Our churches need the King's agenda. Our families need the King's agenda.

We've put together a three-part plan to direct us to heal the divisions and strive for unity as we move toward the goal of truly being one nation under God. This three-part plan calls us to assemble with others in unity, to address the issues that divide us, and to act together for social impact. Following this plan, we will see individuals, families, churches, and communities transformed as we follow God's kingdom agenda in every area of our lives. You can request this plan by emailing info@tonyevans.org or by going online to tonyevans.org.

In many major cities, drivers can take a loop to the other side of the city when they don't want to head straight through downtown. This loop takes them close enough to the city center so they can see its towering buildings and skyline but not close enough to actually experience it.

This is precisely what we, as a culture, have done with God. We have put Him on the "loop" of our personal, family, church, and community lives. He's close enough to be at hand should we need Him in an emergency but far enough away that He can't be the center of who we are. We want God on the "loop," not the King of the Bible who comes downtown into the very heart of our ways. And as we have seen in our own lives and in the lives of others, leaving God on the "loop" brings about dire consequences.

But when we make God and His rule the centerpiece of all we think, do, or say, we experience Him in the way He longs for us to experience Him. He wants us to be kingdom people with kingdom minds set on fulfilling His kingdom's purposes. He wants us to pray, as Jesus did, "Not My will, but Thy will be done" because His is the kingdom, the power, and the glory.

There is only one God, and we are not Him. As King and Creator, God calls the shots. Only when we align ourselves under His comprehensive hand do we access His full power and authority in all spheres of life: personal, familial, ecclesiastical, and government.

As we learn how to govern ourselves under God, we then transform the institutions of family, church, and society using a biblically based kingdom worldview.

Under Him, we touch heaven and change earth.

To achieve our goal, we use a variety of strategies, approaches, and resources for reaching and equipping as many people as possible.

Broadcast Media

Millions of individuals experience *The Alternative with Dr. Tony Evans*, a daily broadcast on nearly 1,400 radio outlets and in over 130 countries. The broadcast can also be seen on several television networks and is available online at tonyevans.org. As well, you can listen to or view the daily broadcast by downloading the Tony Evans app for free in the App Store. Over 30,000,000 message downloads/streams occur each year.

Leadership Training

The *Tony Evans Training Center* (TETC) facilitates a comprehensive discipleship platform, which provides an educational program that embodies the ministry philosophy of Dr. Tony Evans as expressed through the kingdom agenda. The training courses focus on leadership development and discipleship in the following five tracks:

- Bible & Theology
- Personal Growth
- Family and Relationships
- Church Health and Leadership Development
- Society and Community Impact Strategies

The TETC program includes courses for both local and online students. Furthermore, TETC programming includes course work for non-student attendees. Pastors, Christian leaders, and Christian laity—both local and at a distance—can seek out the Kingdom Agenda Certificate for personal, spiritual, and professional development. For more information, visit tonyevanstraining.org.

Kingdom Agenda Pastors (KAP) provides a viable network for like-minded pastors who embrace the kingdom agenda philosophy. Pastors have the opportunity to go deeper with Dr. Tony Evans as they are given greater biblical knowledge, practical applications, and resources to impact individuals, families, churches, and communities. KAP welcomes senior and associate pastors of all churches. KAP also offers an annual KAP Summit each year in Dallas with intensive seminars, workshops, and resources. For more information, visit: kafellowship.org.

Pastors' Wives Ministry, founded by Dr. Lois Evans, provides counsel, encouragement, and spiritual resources for pastors' wives as they serve with their husbands in the ministry. A primary focus of the ministry is the KAP Summit, where senior pastors' wives are offered a safe place to reflect, renew, and relax, along with training in personal development, spiritual growth, and care for their emotional and physical well-being. For more information, visit loisevans.org.

Kingdom Community Impact

The outreach programs of The Urban Alternative seek to provide positive impact on individuals, churches, families, and communities through a variety of ministries. We see these efforts as necessary to our calling as a ministry and essential to the communities we serve. With training on how to initiate and maintain programs to adopt schools; provide homeless services; and partner toward unity and justice with the local police precincts, which creates a connection between the police and our community, we, as a ministry, live out God's kingdom agenda according to our *Kingdom Strategy for Community Transformation*.

The *Kingdom Strategy for Community Transformation* is a three-part plan that equips churches to have a positive impact on their communities for the kingdom of God. It also provides numerous practical suggestions for how this three-part plan can be implemented in your community, and it serves as a blueprint for unifying churches around the common goal of creating a better world for all of us. For more information, visit tonyevans.org, then click on the link to access the 3-Point Plan.

The *National Church Adopt-a-School Initiative* (NCAASI) prepares churches across the country to impact communities by using public schools as the primary vehicle for effecting positive social change in urban youth and families. Leaders of churches, school districts, faith-based organizations, and other nonprofit organizations are equipped with the knowledge and tools to forge partnerships and build strong social service delivery systems. This training is based on the comprehensive church-based community impact strategy conducted by Oak Cliff Bible Fellowship. It addresses such areas as economic development, education, housing, health revitalization, family renewal, and racial reconciliation. We assist churches in tailoring the model to meet specific needs of their communities while simultaneously addressing the spiritual and moral frame of reference. Training events are held annually in the Dallas area at Oak Cliff Bible Fellowship. For more information, visit churchadoptaschool.org.

Athlete's Impact (AI) exists as an outreach both into and through the sports arena. Coaches can be the most influential factor in young people's lives, even ahead of their parents. With the growing rise of fatherlessness in our culture, more young people are looking to their coaches for guidance, character development, meeting practical needs, and hope. Athletes fall just after coaches on the influencer scale. Whether professional or amateur, they influence younger athletes and kids within their spheres of impact. Knowing this, we aim to equip and train coaches and athletes on how to live out and utilize their God-given roles for the benefit of the kingdom. We aim to do this through our iCoach App as well as through resources such as *The Playbook: A Life Strategy Guide for Athletes*. For more information, visit icoachapp.org.

Tony Evans Films ushers in positive life change through compelling video-shorts, animation, and feature-length films. We seek to build kingdom disciples through the power of story; use a variety of platforms for viewer consumption and have more than 100,000,000 digital views; and merge video-shorts and film with relevant Bible study materials to bring people to the saving knowledge of Jesus Christ and to strengthen the body of Christ worldwide. Tony Evans Films released its first feature-length film, *Kingdom Men Rising*, in April 2019 in over 800 theaters nationwide and in partnership with Lifeway Films. The second release, *Journey with Jesus*, is in partnership with RightNow Media.

Resource Development

By providing a variety of published materials, we are fostering lifelong learning partnerships with the people we serve. Dr. Evans has authored more than 125 unique titles based on over 50 years of preaching—in booklet, book, or Bible-study format. He also holds the honor of writing the first full-Bible commentary by an African American. *The Tony Evans Study Bible* was released in 2019, and it sits in permanent display as a historic release in the Museum of the Bible in Washington, D.C.

For more information and a complimentary copy of Dr. Evans's devotional newsletter, call (800) 800-3222; write to TUA at P.O. Box 4000, Dallas, TX, 75208; or visit us online at:

www.tonyevans.org

YOUR *Eternity* IS OUR *Priority*

At The Urban Alternative, eternity is our priority—for the individual, the family, the church and the nation. The 45-year teaching ministry of Tony Evans has allowed us to reach a world in need with:

The Alternative – Our flagship radio program brings hope and comfort to an audience of millions on over 1,300 radio outlets across the country.

tonyevans.org – Our library of teaching resources provides solid Bible teaching through the inspirational books and sermons of Tony Evans.

Tony Evans Training Center – Experience the adventure of God's Word with our online classroom, providing at-your-own-pace courses for your PC or mobile device.

Tony Evans app – Packed with audio and video clips, devotionals, Scripture readings and dozens of other tools, the mobile app provides inspiration on-the-go.

Explore God's kingdom today.
Live for more than the moment.
Live for *eternity*.

tonyevans.org

Life is busy,
but Bible study is still possible.

a **portable**
seminary

Explore the kingdom.
Anytime, anywhere.

tonyevanstraining.org

*Subscription model

To learn more about Harvest House books and
to read sample chapters, visit our website:

www.HarvestHousePublishers.com

HARVEST HOUSE PUBLISHERS
EUGENE, OREGON